Preston North End

Preston North End

The Glory Years Remembered

Mike Prestage

The Breedon Books
Publishing Company
Derby

First published in Great Britain in 2000 by
The Breedon Books Publishing Company Limited
Breedon House, 3 The Parker Centre, Derby, DE21 4SZ.

ISBN 1 85983 199 0

Printed and bound by Butler & Tanner Ltd., Selwood Printing Works,
Caxton Road, Frome, Somerset.

Colour separations and jacket printing by
GreenShires Group Ltd., Leicester.

Contents

The author wishes to thank all those former Preston North End players, and supporters, who spared the time to share with him their memories of this great club. Thanks are also due to Ian Rigby, secretary of the ex-players' association and author of the ground-breaking statistical work on the club.

Introduction

IN THE Fifties, Preston North End established themselves as one of the leading teams in English football. The seeds of their rise had been sown in the post-war years, despite the hiccup of a brief spell in the Second Division. Their success came at a time when the austerity of the war years was beginning to lift and football was enjoying huge popularity. In an age before television, football was the leisure escape of the masses and crowds flocked in numbers never seen before or since. Indeed, for all the hype the Premiership generates today, there were twice as many paying customers in the game's glory years in the post-war era when 40 million supporters filed through the Football League clubs' turnstiles in a season.

Nowhere was the game more an ingrained part of the social fabric than in the industrial towns of Lancashire. And it was not just the large city clubs of Manchester United and City, Liverpool and Everton that led the way. The small mill town clubs made an indelible mark in this period and Preston North End were among them, a force to be reckoned with.

The legendary Tom Finney led the team. Now one of the soccer knights, of course, and properly titled Sir Tom, he was not just the greatest player Preston North End have produced in their long and proud history, but can lay claim to being among the greatest players to have worn the England jersey. He was an iconic player who could lift North End to levels where they could compete with the best in the land. And compete they did. From the post-war years to their last great hurrah when, with Sir Tom retired, they then made another trip to Wembley for an FA Cup Final in 1964.

Although the club were by then in the Second Division, they still showed that, on their day, they were a team to fear. And during Preston's golden age in the Fifties, they reached an FA Cup Final and were twice runners-up in the League.

Perhaps an over reliance on the mercurial talents of Finney was the club's undoing. They came so near to winning some silverware in the post-war years and yet never quite achieved it. For Finney there was to be no Wembley glory in the manner of that other soccer knight, Sir Stanley Matthews, who finally collected his winners' medal at the third attempt in a famous victory against Bolton Wanderers in 1953. Finney, at the end of an illustrious career with North End that spanned more than 20 years and included 442 League games, would collect only a Second Division championship winners' medal and a wartime Cup winners' medal.

There was great debate at the time as to who was the better player, Tom Finney or Stanley Matthews. It is a topic of conversation that can still occupy football fans of a certain generation. Yet if it sparked rivalry between the two sets of supporters, the two great servants of the England side were above such dialogue.

Sir Tom Finney said: "We didn't meet too often, but the times I saw him as a friend was when we were travelling down together to England training sessions and before international matches. We would talk about the game in general. We would also take the opportunity to discuss full-backs we played against. We'd talk about them and swop notes on their strengths and weaknesses. There was no great rivalry, I think what the game is sadly lacking today is a player like Matthews with the skills and tremendous pace to take on two or three defenders and get past them." He was too modest to say it, but another Finney in an England shirt nowadays wouldn't go amiss either.

Talking about the era in which he reigned, he said that there were many outstanding players and the maximum wage ensured they were not all at a handful of clubs. Also, because everybody was on the same wage irrespective of whether they were internationals or star players, and squads were settled, it helped generate a good team spirit among the players themselves. Finney began his first-team career earning £12 a week, and when it ended in 1960 he was on £20.

He said: "To my knowledge nobody was paid more. We heard about clubs where players were given back-handers as part of transfer deals, but that was all. After five years with the club you were entitled to a benefit as a reward for your services. Nowadays, of course, the financial rewards are huge and it is exceptional for a player to stay with a single club, but in the Fifties there was no financial incentive to move."

As a player who was frequently on the receiving end of some rough treatment from defenders keen to nullify his skills, Finney believes the game in his day was much tougher with far less protection from the referees. "It was a harder game in those days. For one thing tackling from behind was legal. The centre-half or full-back could take the player, the ball and everything else and it was legitimate. The game was far more physical. There are so many red and yellow cards around today. It is hard for defenders to make a proper tackle and that is an art that has largely been lost."

However, he never worried about who he was going to be playing against. One suspects it was more likely to be the full-back or centre-half who had the unenviable task of marking him who would be having sleepless nights. Finney said: "I didn't fear anyone, but on the other side of the coin there were a few players I enjoyed playing against because I always seemed to do well against them. It was a question of weighing up the strengths and weaknesses of who you were up against. As a professional player I think you had to have tremendous confidence in your own ability and not bother about the opposition. I just enjoyed getting out there and playing football."

The name of Preston has been carried through the football-playing world, thanks to the glories of its football team and the international players who have come through its ranks. If the fortunes of the club may have waned along with that of the town, then there is perhaps hope for both in the future. Lifting the Second Division championship in the first season of the new millennium has put North End back on the glory trail and, who knows, the Premiership may not be far from their grasp. Major improvements have been made to their Deepdale ground and supporters are starting to return in greater numbers. Not yet to the levels of the Fifties, but given time and a little success, perhaps they will. Soon the leading clubs may be again making the trip to Deepdale and perhaps with the same trepidation of their forebears in the post-war years.

The game still excites passions in the town and recent success has brought back memories of past triumphs. Finney is still connected with the club in his role as president and his continuing presence provides a link between the past and the future. Nobody has been more delighted with the club's recent success than its greatest player.

North End legend Willie Cunningham explained that in his day the game was a far cry from the glamour lifestyles enjoyed by players in the modern era. Not for him an expensive sports car to whisk him on his way when the game was over. Early in his career, when he played for Dunfermline Athletic, the vagaries of the public transport system meant he didn't always manage to get home from away games.

He explained: "I was working down the mine and playing for Dunfermline for £3 a week, which was a good bonus on top of my wage as a miner. I lived at a village called Fordale and used to catch a tramcar to Dunfermline. I remember a match against Airdrie when I caught the bus from Dunfermline. The service wasn't that regular and at the final whistle I had to dash to try to catch the last bus. The reality for a footballer in those days was a world away from today. I can't imagine many modern professionals sprinting for the last bus or combining their career with a job down the pit. One thing's for sure, such a punishing regime made certain I was fit."

Players also had little bargaining power. Some might argue that nowadays the pendulum has swung too far the other way, but Cunningham recalls that, in his day, players had very little say in their future or any clout to get a better financial deal. The maximum wage ensured a limit on the money a player could earn. It meant teams had a settled look about them because there was little point in changing clubs with the money the same everywhere. There was often not a nice percentage of any transfer fee to be pocketed by the player either. Certainly that was the case for Cunningham.

The man who would play over 440 League and Cup games for Preston between 1949 and 1963, as well as winning eight caps for Scotland, remembers his first reaction when the Dunfermline manager called him in to say he was being sold to North End. "Where the hell is Preston?" was the defender's response. Looking back he recalls: "We knew the English clubs and it was always an ambition to play south of the border, but where some of the places were on a map I couldn't have told you. I couldn't believe North End were interested in signing me. Dunfermline were paid £5,000 and I didn't get a penny. I thought it was wrong then and I still think it was wrong. I argued about it but it didn't get me anywhere. I tried to get a pay rise when I arrived at Deepdale, but that wasn't forthcoming either."

It has all changed nowadays and the player thinks that player power has now got out of hand. The modern professional has lost touch with the supporters. Indeed, the importance of the ordinary fan has been undermined by the rise of the corporate clients and the value of merchandising to the bigger clubs. Much of the spirit of being involved with a club in the Fifties has now gone, he believes. The loss affects both the players and the fans.

He said: "We didn't get paid too well but nowadays I think the players are robbing the paying public. It has all gone too far. How can anybody be getting in excess of £40,000 a week to play football? The money being earned is obscene. I am sure that football is in danger of pricing itself out of the market. The whole thing is ridiculous and those in power will only realise when it is too late."

Although the money in his playing days was poor compared to that of today's stars, he makes clear it still was higher than the average working man's take home pay. "I enjoyed playing football in the Fifties and it was a good life. I think the supporters appreciated the game more and we had a good crowd and it was a good bunch of lads in the team. Because everybody was on the same money, there wasn't any discontent over who was earning what in the dressing-room. We were all the same. The maximum wage has few advantages, but that was certainly one. There were some great players around and we had one in Tom Finney."

Joe Dunn, who played for North End for ten years from 1951, believes the football in the Fifties was more entertaining. This was largely because the formations deployed, with five forwards, ensured it was an attacking game that produced many high-scoring matches. There was also a passionate interest in the game in towns like Preston where supporting the local football club was the main leisure pastime for many. Certainly in those towns there was far less interest in supporting the glamour clubs like Manchester United, Chelsea and Arsenal than there is today.

He puts into perspective the money players earned when he says that at the end of his career he was on £20 a week, while a worker at nearby Leyland Motors might be on £10. The money didn't matter when it came to a career choice for Dunn, though. He had always wanted to be a professional footballer and was just delighted to fulfil his ambition.

He said: "There were five brothers and we all played professional football, three of us for Clyde, one for Celtic and one for Hearts. The funny thing was, our father was a coal miner and he couldn't kick a ball across the road, but all the family went on to play football. It was a gift we must have got from somewhere."

He recalls that the social life at Preston was good and the players socialised together. Most played golf and some played snooker. The club was very strict on a no-drinking policy and anyone caught in a pub would be hauled over the coals in the office the following morning. It was a policy which Dunn supported because footballers are professional sportsmen and alcohol and sporting prowess don't go well together. The management also argued that seeing senior players drinking would set a bad example to the younger players.

It is always the case that the sporting memories of our childhood are the ones that stay with us most vividly. Later generations of teams and players have always to compete with the sepia-tinted images of those early years when everything is new and exciting. Many can recall key incidents that established the football team in their hearts and guaranteed a lifetime of support through thick and thin. A stunning victory, a sweetly-taken goal, a favourite personality or the heartbreak of defeat can all be moments that trigger a passion for football and the local team. Few, though, can rival the moment that ensured Preston were to be a feature of Roland Jessop's life.

He explains: "My brother Bill was on the ground staff at Preston and when we won the FA Cup in 1938 the sports teacher at school asked if the kids could see the Cup. It would never happen now but my brother brought it home and said I could take it to school, but I had to look after it. Because we had a lot of Scottish players, there was still the white heather that had been sent down for good luck, which was used to trim the Cup after the match. You can imagine my pride as a ten-year-old, walking down the road with the FA Cup partly wrapped in brown paper. The reaction at school was tremendous and I was the centre of all the attention. The school received two complimentary tickets for Preston matches and I got one nearly every week after that."

Once hooked as a committed Preston fan, he enjoyed the humour on the terraces in the post-war years and the fact that fans appreciated good football, whichever team was playing it. It was real fun. He remembers a story about a wartime game when a visitor to Preston was on the terraces. He noticed figures in army blouses and trousers, but with a big yellow dot on their back. The visitor asked who they were and was told they were Italian prisoners-of-war. He asked: "Do they allow them to watch the game then?" To which a local replied: "Oh yes, at Preston it's part of the punishment."

Jessop recalls that this was a time when the crowds were so large that there was always the danger of being locked out if you weren't there early enough. Average attendances of more than 30,000 ensured a terrific atmosphere. There was no mindless chanting, but everyone seemed to be a comedian. The idea of supporting another team never crossed their minds.

Football was also to play another significant role in his life. Never one for slavish tribal loyalties when it came to football, he would go to watch a match at Blackpool if Preston were playing away. And, of course, he went to the great derby matches between the two. It was on the terraces at Bloomfield Road that he met his future wife, Kathleen, who went to the games with her family. Everybody had their favourite spot and over the course of a season the two got to know each other. True love, though, was not enough to change his allegiance from North End to the Seasiders.

Having his brother Bill on the playing staff gave Jessop an insight into life behind the scenes at Deepdale and he believes the players, particularly those outside the first team, were not treated well. The status of a professional footballer was not high. The working conditions were strict.

He has a number of anecdotes which show how different life was for the professional footballer in the post-war years compared to the pampered lifestyles their counterparts enjoy today.

He said: "I remember talking to a centre-forward called Alex Halston and we forgot the time. Suddenly he dashed for the Deepdale entrance, but at bang on nine o'clock they locked the gate and he ended up getting fined for missing a day's work. That's how strict they were. Another time I remember Bill coming home with tar on him. The young players had been recruited to tar the roof of the stand. At other times they might be weeding the terraces. They put them to work, it wasn't all playing football."

The attitude of the club when players returned after the war prompted an exodus of young players, of which Bill Jessop was part. Roland said: "It wasn't just the strict way they were treated but the attitude of those in charge. The president used to arrive wearing starched, wing collars and act like they were children. These were men who had returned from fighting in the war. They might have been lads when they went but they came back as men. Bill went to Stockport and then had six seasons at Oldham."

Veteran supporter Wilf Wareing misses the camaraderie among the fans that used to be such an enjoyable part of going to football in the Fifties, especially when it was some of the Lancashire derbies. "I remember seeing Preston play Bolton Wanderers and being sat near the cinder track that used to run around their pitch. Their fans would joke that their full-backs, Tommy Banks and Roy Hartle, would dump a few of our lads on the cinder track and often they did. They were a strong defensive side, Wanderers. But among the fans it was all taken in the right spirit. You could have a laugh and a joke with each other. People weren't blinkered in their views. They'd talk about Tom Finney and his talent and we knew what Nat Lofthouse was capable of for them. If there were arguments, they were in good spirit. Not having segregation and barriers added to the atmosphere."

And he added: "In the late Fifties when we were League runners-up, we were feared. Preston were up there with the Arsenals and the Manchester Uniteds. It was not just North End. In this part of the world we had Burnley, Bolton Wanderers and Blackpool, who on their day could beat anybody. This part of Lancashire was a hotbed for soccer."

Marian Bell, now 75, used to go in a family group to watch Preston in the post-war years and has been a devoted fan since. Those days in the Forties and Fifties represent the highlight of her football watching as crowds flocked in their thousands.

She said: "Football in that era was special. It brought the whole community together and because there was no violence it could be a family day out. We used to catch two buses to the ground and got there early to ensure a front row in the Paddock. The whole family went. Going to the football was like an institution. The same people were around you every week and you swopped coffee and biscuits. Now money has taken over and it isn't as enjoyable as it used to be. Preston were a good footballing side in those days and, of course, we had Tom Finney."

She adds: "It's easy to forget that the games were played in conditions they wouldn't dream of playing football in now and with a heavy leather ball. Some of the players nowadays aren't fit to lace the boots of the stars of the post-war years. I remember seeing Willie Cunningham having to try to play in a deep rut that was gouged in one pitch."

She recalls that in this era the players were no different than the supporters and were seen around the town. Bobby Beattie used to take his children to the same school as her kids. The money for footballers was not that much better than what everybody else earned. Players and fans were part of the same community and enjoyed similar lifestyles.

Walter Horan, better known throughout Lancashire as the

comedian Wandering Walter, who was a popular performer on the club circuit and at sportsmen's dinners, had first been taken to Deepdale in the Thirties and he remembers the celebrations that surrounded Preston's FA Cup win in 1938 when a last-minute George Mutch penalty was the only goal in a win against Huddersfield Town. As a ten-year-old standing on the terraces he was given an insight into the passions football can generate in a game against Grimsby Town when winger Jimmy Dougal was kicked in the jaw by the 'keeper and his father screamed: "You dirty bugger." Horan explained: "I had never heard my dad swear before. It was quite out of character."

By the Fifties he was a committed fan and he says of this period in football history: "Preston has always been a football town and a few good results is enough to generate excitement. I was once asked if rugby league would ever take off here and I said it wouldn't. Those of us watching football in the Fifties were privileged to witness open, skilful football. There was none of this possession game. It was a standard we will never see again. I have to confess I can't be bothered with football nowadays."

After The War

THE declaration of war in September 1939 brought an end to League football with only three games in the season played. It was seven years later when the League programme resumed and, as though frozen in time, the fixture list that was so abruptly interrupted by the outbreak of hostilities was revived. Many players had guested for other teams during the war, but all who were resurrecting their careers now returned to their original clubs.

Everybody was glad to see the return of League football. Preston were a Division One side and for the first two seasons after the restart they were to maintain a healthy, top-of-the-table position, finishing seventh in the top flight in both campaigns. For many of the players, some of the best years of their football careers had been lost and now there was just relief at being back and playing football.

For the opening game of the 1946-47 season there were four players on the team sheet who had been first-team regulars before the war. Andy Beattie, Bill Shankly, Jimmy Dougal and Bobby Beattie brought experience to the side that now included a young Tom Finney, who had won rave reviews playing wartime football before Army duties saw him posted overseas. A public starved of football for so long, and for whom football was a relatively cheap entertainment, swelled the terraces at Deepdale. There were more than 25,000 there for the opening game of the season with the highest home attendance a Boxing Day fixture with Chelsea, which attracted 40,167 paying customers. The biggest crowd the Preston players performed before was a sixth-round FA Cup-tie against Charlton Athletic, which drew a crowd of 56,340.

Finney said: "It was true to say that a lot of teams in those early years after the war were unknown quantities. They were composed of players who had been around pre-war and youngsters who had matured during the seven years when there was no League football. It was good for us younger players at Preston to be playing alongside footballers with a great deal of experience. If you were prepared to listen and learn from the older players, then they were willing to pass on whatever information and advice they felt was necessary. They had no time for anybody who felt they knew it all. I used to sit and listen because they all talked a lot of sense. People like Bill Shankly and Andy Beattie had lost the prime of their careers."

During his Army career serving in Egypt for two years, Finney had played football for a side called the Wanderers, which was composed of mainly professional players and was a wonderful experience. Later he played for the Eighth Army team in Italy. It was nothing, though, compared to the thrill of being in League action. He recalls the first two seasons saw Preston turn in some reasonable performances. For players like Bill Shankly it provided a last hurrah before their playing careers drew to a close.

Shankly had played in the 1938 Cup Final win sealed with a George Mutch penalty in the 89th minute and his experience and talent at wing-half in the years after the war were invaluable to Preston's cause. He had a passion for the game both on and off the field. Fans in the street who stopped to chat football could find themselves embroiled in hour-long conversations on the finer points of the game. Unfortunately, like many players of his ilk, the fiery nature of Shankly's play and his tackling ability tended to obscure his passing and tactical skill. Much, though, that the young Finney achieved on the wing was possible because of the work of Shankly behind him.

He joined Preston in July 1933, from Carlisle United for a fee of £500, and would play for the club until 1949. He had made the journey south of the border after being spotted playing for a junior team in Scotland, Glenbuck Cherrypickers. Shankly played 296 League games for North End in a career interrupted by the war and also appeared in a record 43 successive Cup-ties for the club. The hostilities also limited his international appearances, although he won five caps for Scotland. He was, of course, to find even greater fame as a manager with Liverpool.

Walter Horan explained that before showbusiness became his career, he had entertained hopes of being a professional footballer and during his younger years he was on the books at Preston North End as a goalkeeper, having answered an advertisement for interested players to go down to the ground for a trial. His career in the years immediately after the war had to survive an accident with a lorry while he was working as a grocery delivery boy and was knocked off his bike injuring his foot.

He recalls: "I reported to Deepdale for my first game and was told I had half an hour to wait. Suddenly in came Bill Shankly, who was playing for the Reserves. I said: 'Hello Mr Shankly,' and he replied: 'It's Bill, the name's Bill.' He'd come in to see the groundsman because he had given instructions that the grass shouldn't be cut. He turned to me and joked: 'I like the grass long, so if I'm having a bad game I can duck down and hide.' As soon as the game kicked-off he called for the ball and passed it to me so I could get an early feel of it and to help me settle. It's one of many great memories."

Horan recalls that Shankly was a tough player with no little skill, but he also took on board another role. It was one that was to be inherited by his successor Tommy Docherty, a player in the same mould. "If there was a particularly bad foul on Tom Finney, then Shankly would bide his time for a little while and then go looking for the offending player. Protecting Tom wasn't part of his job, but it was a task he took on. Shankly was a great servant to Preston and when his career came to a close he thought he would get a job with the club as a coach and he was bitterly disappointed that they didn't give him one."

He said there was a good social life at the club, although not many drank alcohol. Willie Cunningham was a keen dancer and would go to local halls with his wife. Joe Dunn was a regular at the Olympic Café in town where he was very popular with the ladies. He also remembers a story which Bobby Beattie told him. After a game, he and Shankly had hired a car and gone to Blackpool for the night.

While Beattie would enjoy a drink and a dance, Shankly would set off to try to find a cinema showing a James Cagney movie. "As they were coming home around midnight, the lights of a tram were heading towards them and Bill, who was the passenger, started screaming: 'Get off the road, get off the road,' at the tram, not realising it was on fixed rails. Fortunately Bobby did and swerved out of the way."

In the 1946-47 season, Horan was playing in the Reserves against Bolton Wanderers at Burnden Park and thought this was his first big step on the ladder to the top. He was told a perk for reserve players was tickets for family and friends and he asked for a couple for his dad and brother. The reply was short and to the point: "Look lad, you've only just started in football. If your dad and brother won't pay to watch you play, then how can you expect any other bugger to."

His first game was not an auspicious start. "We lost 4-0 and the gaffer said we were lucky to get nil. It was a bit harsh because Bolton had some good young players coming through the ranks. I remember Malcolm Barrass played and he went on to be an international centre-half. However, I was still in the team for a game against Manchester United Reserves at Old Trafford. The pitch was in good condition, but the stands had been bombed in the war. We changed in an air-raid shelter. I was beginning to feel at home in the side now."

The maximum wage ensured that clubs could afford to carry large squads. Horan remembers it was not just on the wages that Preston cut corners to save money. He recalls that on away games there was no meal provided, but one of the directors was a butcher and he brought a box of pies and a box of ham sandwiches. He also received half a crown (13p) appearance money. His fledgling career in the Reserves was not to last beyond the arrival of a bigger, more experienced lad. He did play a few games for the 'A' team, but hopes of a professional career were over and from now on it would be as a supporter that Horan followed Preston.

A treasured memory, though, is of a training session where as a young goalkeeper he faced Tom Finney coming off the wing in full flight. He was serving in the RAF but would write to the club when he was home on leave and turn out for the lower sides. "Any young 'keeper suffering constipation only had to play against Tom if he was looking for an easy cure. When he turned it on he was incredible and it is something to look back on and say I kept goal against him, even though it was only in training."

Although during the war the Football League programme was suspended, there had been some football during those years. Finney's wartime footballing exploits for North End included a Wembley appearance and a Cup win. In the 1940-41 season Preston, as northern champions, met Arsenal, the southern victors, at Wembley and the game ended 1-1. It meant a replay at Ewood Park, home of Blackburn Rovers, where Preston triumphed 2-1. Football at Deepdale, though, was soon to come to an end with the ground being taken over by the military and used as a reception centre for prisoners-of-war.

Finney recalls: "Playing in the wartime Final was a fantastic experience especially as it involved a trip to Wembley. I remember standing in the tunnel and listening to the crowd. It was deafening, even though there had been a limit put on numbers because of the blitz. Arsenal were favourites but we had some of the players from the Thirties era like Shankly, the Beattie brothers and Tom Smith, and I was very fortunate to come into a side with their talent and experience. I was playing against the then England captain Eddie Hapgood and had a pretty good game according to the press reports. We drew 1-1 and then beat them at Blackburn. We each got 15 shillings' worth of wartime savings certificates and a bronze medal which I still have. It was a good start to my career, but for the next three years I had Army postings abroad."

The programme in 1946-47 season began with a home game against Leeds United. It took only four minutes for Preston to score the first goal of the new era with debutant centre-forward Willie McIntosh making the most of a perfect pass from Finney to give the goalkeeper no chance with the shot. The crowd, who had been anxious to see what the young Finney could do in League action, was left in no doubt as to his prowess in the 18th minute when he deftly beat a defender to create the opening for himself which he exploited for Preston's second goal. It was a superb solo effort that had the crowd roaring. Leeds pulled a goal back, but Scottish international Jimmy Dougal made it safe with a goal in the 75th minute, despite a second for Leeds in the closing minutes.

Preston made too many slip-ups to seriously challenge for the title and were to finish ten points behind eventual winners, Liverpool. However, when the side clicked they could produce an avalanche of goals to the delight of their supporters. An example came in the FA Cup where Barnsley arrived for a fourth-round tie full of confidence. At half-time there was no score, but then it was the turn of the Shankly, Finney and Andy McLaren combination to work their magic on the right, aided by the man of the match Bob Beattie, whose clever passing created numerous openings. Six goals were the result as the Yorkshire side were swept away and their hopes of achieving at least a replay were shattered. It brought back memories of the 1938 FA Cup campaign that ended with glory at Wembley. On the terraces there were hopes that the success could be repeated, particularly if North End continued to produce such irresistible form. There were four goals in nine minutes and, despite scoring six, Preston squandered many other chances. Barnsley were lucky not to have suffered a reverse in double figures.

The Cup hopes, though, were not to last. After a 2-0 victory against Sheffield Wednesday, in a game that was three times postponed due to weather, Preston faced a trip to London to meet Charlton, who were near the bottom of the League. In a controversial game the northern side lost 2-1 to a hotly-disputed goal. Having already rejected Preston appeals for a penalty, the referee then allowed a ball that appeared to be out of play to be crossed for Gordon Hurst to score. The players were incensed, but their protests fell on deaf ears. Preston were themselves guilty of missing some clear chances and a game they deserved to have won was lost. Charlton Athletic, having cleared such a difficult hurdle, were to go on to win the Cup, beating Preston's neighbours Burnley 1-0 in the Final after extra-time.

If losing in the Cup to Charlton was bad enough, a greater misfortune to befall North End had occurred two weeks before. There is a great rivalry between all the Lancashire clubs, but for Preston their near-neighbours Blackpool are the main protagonists. To lose by four goals was bad enough, but at the hands of the Seasiders was a memory that would haunt Preston fans of a certain generation for years to come.

Blackpool had lost 2-0 at Deepdale, but now gained sweet revenge with an emphatic 4-0 victory that had the added bonus of taking them above Preston in the League. On a snow-covered pitch they were faster and more effective and took their opportunities when they arose. By contrast, Preston squandered what openings they created for themselves. Finney was the best of the forwards on either side and twice came close to scoring, on one occasion hitting the post and on another knocking-out an opponent with his shot. However, he did miss a penalty. Preston also had two goals disallowed. That a 4-0 score flattered Blackpool was little consolation to the Preston fans as they streamed from the ground.

A poor close to the season, in which Preston managed to win only three of the last 13 games, meant a seventh-place finish, but there were high hopes among fans that the following year would be better if the Lilywhites could only manage to keep the goals out as well as they banged them in at the other end.

Sadly, it was not to be the case. Preston had the unusual achievement, for a side that finished as high as seventh, of conceding more goals than they scored. A 7-0 hiding by Blackpool at Deepdale in the last match of the season certainly didn't help the cause as Preston caught a backlash from the beaten Cup Finalists who were looking to put behind them their Wembley defeat against Manchester United the week before. For the visiting fans it was the best consolation prize they could hope for to end the season. For the home fans, those trips to Blackpool for the summer holidays would lose some of their attraction.

The only crumb of comfort for Preston fans was that North End had managed to come away with the points on their visit to Bloomfield Road in December. In those days, supporters were often unable to travel the long distances to far-flung grounds for away matches. It was a time that preceded motorways and money was tight for many people. There were also frequently heavy work commitments. Yet the short journey to the seaside resort of Blackpool was a popular outing well within the means of many. Scoring a win, even by 1-0, over their rivals was the perfect prelude to a night out in the resort before catching the train home.

If the 7-0 drubbing was to be the low point of the season for the Lilywhites, then the side were to be on the right side of a seven-goal score when Derby County were the visitors. Indeed, the game produced one of the most exciting Deepdale has witnessed.

Derby were unbeaten in their previous ten games, but that record was set to be ended in glorious style. The fans had barely settled in their places on the terraces when there was a rush of goals. Three came in six minutes, with two of them from the penalty spot. Derby drew first blood when Jack Howe converted the penalty after Emlyn Williams was adjudged to have handled a Raich Carter header. Angus Morrison got the second for the visitors with a shot that went in off the post. Derby were well on top, but now it was time for the North End revival. They won a penalty for a foul on Harry Anders, which Shankly converted. A Finney corner headed home by Andy McLaren provided the equaliser, but it was Derby who regained the lead again through Morrison. With the game being played at a frenetic pace, Shankly brought the sides level just before half-time. Morrison duly completed his hat-trick to make it 4-3 and within two minutes Bobby Beattie brought the scores level again. Preston finished the stronger and three goals in the last 15 minutes brought a resounding win and left the supporters breathless.

More than 50 years on Angus Morrison recalls: "There can't be many times a player scores a hat-trick and ends up on the losing side. It was a terrific game and even years later, people in Preston would still talk about it. Certainly I think my performance in that match helped persuade North End to sign me and I arrived the following season. I had no say in the transfer. At Derby they called me in and told me I was going to Preston. I wasn't supposed to know the fee, but they gave me some paperwork and forgot to remove it, so I know Preston paid £8,000. I didn't get a penny, of course."

Morrison's arrival was still a season away. Preston had started the 1947-48 League campaign well with nine wins in their first 12 games, but as their League form faltered, it was left to the Cup to provide the chance of glory. Wins against Millwall and Portsmouth brought a fifth-round tie against Manchester City with Willie McIntosh providing the only goal. The second half of the game against Portsmouth brought a portent for the future with Finney switching to centre-forward as an emergency measure. It was a position he was to take on full-time later in his North End career.

Preston had played every round away from home and when the balls were drawn for the next round it was again an away tie and a return to Maine Road. This time it was Manchester United they faced. Old Trafford had been badly damaged in the blitz and United were using their neighbours' ground for home matches. A huge crowd of 74,243 crammed into the ground to watch the Lancashire derby. In this cauldron Jack Hindle made his first-team debut in the North End goal. There could be no tougher baptism into top-flight football.

Preston had travelled to the same ground in the League a fortnight before and gained a creditable 1-1 draw. Their performance in the Cup was to be more disappointing as they succumbed 4-1 to a Manchester United side that would go on to win the trophy by beating Blackpool at Wembley the following May. North End were establishing a knack of going out to the eventual winners, having done the same with Charlton the previous season. United went all out for attack and it paid off as the Preston defenders struggled to prevent a glut of goals being conceded and the four they scored did not flatter United, such was the edge they had in the match. Too many Preston players had an off day with Shankly strangely out of sorts and Beattie subdued. Finney rarely got the better of the defenders, but the one time he did, his pass split the defence and set Willie McIntosh up for the visitors' only goal. Hindle did not do badly, but the view from the Preston fans was that Gooch would have saved at least a couple of the goals.

An ever-present in the first season of League football, and one of the players frequently overlooked when great servants of Preston North End are recalled, was Billy Scott. A local lad, he was working as a plasterer when he went down for a trial and was taken on. He eventually worked his way up through the 'A' and 'B' teams and then the Reserves before making his League debut against Leeds United on the opening day of the 1946-47 season.

He had, though, played some first-team football during the war when his RAF duties allowed, including being in the 1941 Football League Cup Final side that defeated Arsenal in a replay 2-1 after drawing at Wembley 1-1. Scott had an unsmiling and fearsome demeanour, completed with thick black hair that was low on his brow. A quiet man, he let his football do the talking and he was a quietly efficient full-back who was a superb timer of a tackle.

His family remembers during the war the frequent arrival of telegrams from clubs asking if he could guest for them, including Crewe Alexandra and Chester, which were close to where he was stationed. Scott played more than 200 League games for North End and was an integral part of the promotion-winning side. He would remain at Deepdale until 1954.

He said: "After the war everybody was just glad to have football back, either as players or fans. Football was the main entertainment for the working man. Times were still hard for many and going to watch the game on a Saturday was a release from the routine of work and the restrictions of rationing. It was an affordable day out. We weren't earning a fortune, but it was still more than the factory worker."

Scott recognises times have changed and is unsure whether it is for the better. "I cringe when I hear modern players dictating terms to clubs. In my day we felt happy that we had done enough to earn a bit extra. Once a few of us plucked up the courage to go and speak to manager Will Scott about more money. When we got to his office and put our case, all he said was: 'You're getting big headed. Good morning.' That was that. We all trooped out with our tails between our legs. In those days the clubs were the bosses. Now it seems to be the players who rule the roost."

He knows that he was not always the fans' favourite player. Far from it. But the letters at the time to the local *Lancashire Evening Post* extolling his hard work and commitment to the team showed he had his support among those who appreciated the quiet way he went about his business. Indeed, one correspondent suggested he was a player in the £10,000 bracket. It was a tidy sum in the late Forties and early Fifties. The player himself was not unduly bothered by any criticism from the terraces. "The crowd used to have a go at times but I never used to bother," he said.

The full-back was noted for his tussles with the legendary 'Wizard of Dribble', Stanley Matthews, when arch rivals Blackpool were the visitors and he fared as well as anyone against Matthews. He found the best tactic was to try to force him away from the touchline, but it was easier said than done. "He was a great player and you could only do your best. He wasn't the only one, though. There were a lot of talented players in those days. Matthews was a bit special. He had great skill and you couldn't relax for a minute."

Matthews himself had a particular memory of Preston that featured in a landmark in his career. His first match for Blackpool was a wartime game against the Lilywhites and it ended in defeat. It was to presage many titanic struggles between the two clubs during the Fifties that were, for many fans of both sides, one of the highlights of the season.

For Preston fans, the two seasons of League football after the war had brought plenty of entertainment and if the chase for the silverware had faltered, there was still much to praise in the North End performances. The crowds were still flocking in, with over 40,000 watching the game against Arsenal in September 1947. The resumption of League football had seen Preston rekindle old glories. Alas, it was not to last.

Relegation

AFTER enjoying relative success, Preston North End slipped out of the First Division after losing a relegation battle that went all the way to the last game. The loss of Tom Finney for most of the season was a factor. There was also the departure of Bill Shankly to cope with. For the fans, though, the season was a bitter blow. The old problem of conceding too many goals remained. This time, however, the net was not being hit frequently enough at the other end.

Traditionally in football at this time, consistency in team selection was important. The days of a squad system and rotating the first team were a long way off. Winning teams rarely changed their line-up from one season to the next. In the 1948-49 season, Preston found themselves rarely able to send out the same team from one week to the next. In goal Jimmy Gooch vied with Malcolm Newlands. Due to either injury or loss of form, in no position did one player keep his place through the entire season. At centre-forward, for example, five players all had a spell wearing the number-nine shirt: Willie McIntosh, Harry Jackson, the newly-arrived Angus Morrison, Eddie Brown and, for the last match of the season, Bobby Langton, a signing from Blackburn Rovers.

Langton arrived in a blaze of publicity in August 1948. He was establishing himself as a leading player of the day and the £16,000 paid by Preston was a considerable fee at the time. Langton had already played for England and great things were expected of the outside-left, especially when in his second game for North End, against Manchester City, he scored within seven seconds of the kick-off. However, with relegation his career at Deepdale came to an end after just 55 League games and a respectable tally of 14 goals. He moved to Bolton Wanderers for £20,000, where he stayed until 1953 before he rejoined Blackburn Rovers.

Walter Horan believes Langton suffered because of comparisons with Tom Finney. "Langton was a fine footballer, but playing at outside-left brought its comparisons with Tom and he was never going to be as clever, dynamic or score the goals like Tom Finney. He did have class and if he had stayed a while longer, he would have quickly won the fans over. As it was he was only there for a season."

Horan remembers that as the season wore on, the spectre of relegation loomed ever larger. The first team was being hit by injuries and results were going against the side. He was playing for the 'A' side and was having his own troubles. He injured an ankle in a West Lancashire Cup match against Blackpool as he challenged for a ball with Jackie Mudie, who would later play for Scotland and be an integral part of Blackpool's great side of the Fifties.

Although injured, Horan played on and even managed to save a Mudie penalty in a game that was drawn. However, he was to soon discover that man management was not in vogue in these times. He recalls: "When I came off, the bloke in charge made a beeline for me and said he was unhappy with my performance and would be making a report about me when he got back. I took my boot off and my foot swelled up like a balloon. I don't know how I managed to play the best part of 80 minutes with the injury. At the hospital they said it wasn't broken but it was badly wrenched. Back at Deepdale, nobody wanted to know. That was my last game for Preston."

One of the players to wear the number-nine shirt in the relegation season was Eddie Brown. Although from Preston, he had been educated in the Channel Islands by the De La Salle Christian Brothers as part of his preparation for becoming a monk. However, before he took his vows he decided the life wasn't for him so he returned to his home town and went down to Deepdale where he announced he was a centre-forward. He was taken on to the car park for an impromptu trial.

He said: "They threw a few balls at me and I didn't trap a single one, but I did all right in the sprinting and turning. I was a good runner and in the summer I used to race for money. I once won £5 in a 100-yard sprint where I had to give away nine yards. That was good money in the Forties. A couple of weeks after my trial there was a vacancy in the 'A' team and I scored a hat-trick, so the fact I couldn't trap a ball went out of the window."

He recalls his early days at Deepdale, saying: "It was like an apprenticeship. If you couldn't learn from the likes of Finney and Shankly, you had to be thick. Bill used to walk past where I was staying and we would walk together to the ground and then he would wait after training and we would walk back. He never stopped talking football from the moment he arrived at my door to the time he said goodbye in the evening. He was a football fanatic. It was natter, natter, natter. I think his principle was that if he said enough, some of it would stick. Tom was much quieter and didn't say too much. Tom was the greatest player I have ever seen and to work with him and play alongside him was tremendous. The secret was to listen to Bill and watch Tom. That was the way to improve."

Brown believes they were wonderful days to be playing football and although he had less than three seasons at Deepdale, they were the salad days to be involved in football with huge crowds and a terrific atmosphere. Without television and its endless replays and the experts quick with their damning opinions, there was less criticism of the players and there wasn't the same spotlight on everything they did. The only match reports were in the *Lancashire Evening Post*. The pressure was less, although the crowd did make clear their displeasure if things weren't going well.

He said: "As I was a bit of a showman, playing in those days was like being on the stage with a noisy, partisan audience cheering your every move. And I used to play to the gallery. The sort of gimmicks that are commonplace now were new in the Forties and the crowd loved it. Once when I scored a goal I went to the corner flag and did a pirouette with it. The goal celebrations were because I never knew if I would get another one. It's a wonderful moment when you hit a shot that is going in and you can hear the shout of the crowd. I loved it. Another celebration was to go and kiss a lady behind the goal. Old ones or young ones, it didn't matter. The crowd enjoyed it. I also had a trick of reciting Shakespeare to the opposing goalies to distract them, which used to get them really annoyed. I'd keep out of their way as they started blaspheming oaths. In my career I scored 237 Cup and League goals and I had some fair old celebrations to mark each one."

In their opening eight games, North End managed only two wins with both Manchester City and Burnley doing the double over them. Yet those two wins showed that when the side hit form they could run up big wins and give the fans hope that like the previous two seasons they would be in the upper reaches of the table. There was an impressive 6-1 win at Deepdale against Middlesbrough. Even better, though, was when Preston journeyed to the North East to play Newcastle United and triumphed 5-2. The Lilywhites won only three games on their travels in the season, but this was a magnificent performance.

In front of a crowd of 63,549 roaring them on, Newcastle had the better of the opening exchanges and scored after seven minutes when Andy Donaldson rounded Bill Corbett and his shot beat Malcolm Newlands and was in the Preston net. The visitors soon hit back when a cross by Bobby Beattie was met by McIntosh. Soon Preston, led by Finney, were taking control and their pressure brought its reward with a goal when a Finney corner was met by McLaren's header. Just before half-time the lead was extended when McLaren was left in acres of space and an accurate pass gave him the simplest of chances. After 55 minutes it was 4-1 when the Newcastle goalkeeper parried a McLaren shot to McIntosh. Newcastle pulled a goal back, but the last word went to Preston and it was Finney himself who scored it. As the season wore on, how the Preston fans could only wish for more performances of this quality.

Walter Horan remembers: "The relegation season was a cruel one. We had signed Bobby Langton from Blackburn Rovers and he was highly rated and although Shankly was on his way, everybody was confident about the season, especially as we had some good results early on. The problem was that Tom Finney had a torrid time with muscle injuries and when Jimmy Gooch in goal was injured, the directors, instead of buying an experienced 'keeper, persevered with a reserve. He gave away goals that a fit Gooch would not have conceded."

Gooch was a 'keeper who could turn in some wonderful performances, although he did have his occasional lapses. He was the regular between the posts from August 1947, when he replaced Jack Fairbrother who had been sold to Newcastle United for £7,000. He was to suffer serious injuries, which at times threatened his career, but he had the determination to battle back. In 1947-48, a shoulder injury sustained against Manchester United was aggravated the following week playing against Blackburn Rovers. In only the second game of the relegation season he dislocated his shoulder and needed surgery. Afterwards he was never guaranteed a first-team place. He left in July 1953 to join Bradford City.

As a 'keeper himself, Horan took a keen interest in the men between the posts. He had been a great fan of Fairbrother, who played throughout the first season of post-war League football in 1946-47, only to be transferred as the club cashed in. "Jack's career had been hit by the war and then, when he got his chance, he wasn't here long. Like a lot of fans I was disappointed when he left. I remember he was always smiling. They took the money because they had Jimmy Gooch. I was asked what I thought of Jimmy and I told them he was brave, daring and some might say stupid in some of the things he did. He was good to watch, but he picked up a lot of injuries. There wasn't much protection for the goalkeeper in those days. They were the men on the flying trapeze and in Jimmy's case he tended to fall off a lot."

The reality of First Division life for a struggling side was graphically brought home on October 30, when Manchester United were the visitors. The week before, Preston had achieved a rare away win, overcoming Huddersfield Town, and they approached the game with some confidence, even though this was virtually United's Cup-winning side. North End started well and scored the opening goal when Tommy Bogan feigned to shoot, but instead passed back to Beattie who calmly side-footed the ball into the net.

United, though, always looked threatening and when Newlands failed to hold a corner, the ball fell to Stan Pearson whose shot evaded two defenders guarding the line. Preston were forced into some desperate defence, but they could not keep the Manchester players at bay and by half-time it was 3-1 with Charlie Mitten and Pearson both scoring. In the second half United always looked the more dangerous and tormented the Preston defenders at will and three second-half goals were their reward. The 6-1 defeat would be North End's worst of the season.

With three games of the season remaining, Bolton Wanderers visited Deepdale. Points were vital for both sides, but more so for Preston. Two points would virtually assure Wanderers of First Division safety. Preston's position was more perilous. On the day of the 1949 FA Cup Final between Wolves and Leicester City (who had knocked-out Preston in the fourth round), more than 33,000 ignored the radio commentary from Wembley and were packed on to the Deepdale terraces to cheer Preston on a bright sunny afternoon. There was a nervous start by both sides and North End had two penalty appeals turned down when Langton was shoulder-charged by Lol Hamlett and Brown was sandwiched between Malcolm Barrass and Ralph Banks. The home side had squandered chances until the 37th minute when a pass by Finney found Beattie. Bolton had few chances, but were to gain a point, thanks to the efforts of their England centre-forward Nat Lofthouse whose header from a corner gave Gooch in the Preston net no hope. It was a lost point that Preston were to rue.

The penultimate game was a daunting prospect for Preston, who were locked in a relegation struggle with Sheffield United, Huddersfield Town and Middlesbrough. They had to travel to the recent Cup winners, Wolves, whose 55,000 capacity crowd were in celebratory mood. With no pressure on them other than to entertain, Wolves turned in an exhibition performance, winning 2-1. Finney was on the sidelines for the match with a recurrence of the groin strain that had troubled him for much of the season. He could only watch as his team-mates squandered chances and then, to add insult to injury, Gooch was at fault for the second Wolves goal when he let a Johnny Hancock free-kick from 30 yards out go through his hands. An 87th-minute penalty for Langton was just too late.

It meant that with one game left, Preston had to travel to Liverpool. North End were lying second from bottom with 31 points and anything but a win would see them doomed. Even both points would not guarantee safety. Middlesbrough needed only one point to be sure of staying up and Sheffield United needed only two points and had two games in hand. Huddersfield Town, with two home matches remaining, could also get past the 33-point mark which is the most Preston could hope to achieve. The situation was not hopeless but, of the relegation contenders, North End appeared to be in the worst position.

For the Liverpool game, Finney returned but, even so, desperate fans were working out goal-averages. It was going to be that close, even if Liverpool could be overcome. The omens were not good, with no Preston side having won at Anfield since 1919-20. Finney again showed his versatility by playing at his international position of outside-left. His more usual outside-right berth was occupied by Stanley Matthews for England, and now by Harry Anders for the Liverpool match.

North End made all the opening pressure and Langton had a number of early chances. It was the visitors who were playing all the constructive football. The contingent of fans that had made the journey to support the side witnessed a composed performance with not a hint of nerves or panic about it. Those supporters were certain a goal would come and so it did with Jackie Knight the scorer. In the second half Liverpool strove hard for an equaliser and with the clock ticking down Preston defended desperately. With three minutes to go, Langton missed an open goal when he blasted his shot rather than place it, and it was not until the final moments that the game was made safe when Finney, who had been playing at half speed as the game wore on and his injury took its toll, received a pass from Knight, beat a defender and then cut in to score from a narrow angle. There was not even time to restart the game.

During the contest the news from the other relegation matches was good. However, the football fates were to conspire against

Preston. Middlesbrough achieved the point they needed, and a win for Huddersfield, earned with a quarter of an hour left to play, saw them also scrape clear. Preston finished with 33 points, the same as bottom-of-the-table Sheffield United. They had won promotion 15 years before, but now football outside the top flight was to return to Deepdale.

Tom Finney reveals that the prospect of Second Division football had him pondering his future at Deepdale. "We had some players out with injury during the season and it had been a struggle, but when we were finally relegated it was a bitter blow. For myself, I felt it was going to have some effect on my international career. I spoke to the chairman, Jim Taylor, to voice my concerns and he assured me Preston were going to strengthen the side and he was convinced we were only going to be in the Second Division for a short space of time. Happily, his promises came true."

Eddie Brown remembers: "I was disappointed at being relegated of course, but I was still a young player and it was all new to me. I rather looked on it as part of a learning curve. There was criticism levelled at the players, but I didn't take it too much to heart. In football you have to take the bad times with the good. Nobody goes out to lose, but each season teams get relegated. It is part of a professional player's life."

Walter Horan was behind the scenes at Deepdale in those final weeks and he recalls: "While there is a glimmer of hope that relegation can be avoided, everybody is trying to be positive, but once it is all over there is always a bad atmosphere as the gloom descends. Everybody knew there would be a loss of revenue playing Second Division teams and that cutbacks in the squad might be made. There was a feeling we could bounce back but patience would be required."

Angus Morrison suffered the ignominy of being relegated in his first season with Preston, but he was to play a key role in the promotion success two years later. He was also a member of the 1954 Wembley side. In a career spanning 262 League games, he scored 70 times and was a favourite with the crowd. He has fond memories of his time at the club, although the relegation year was the low point.

He said: "They were a very good club and it was a pleasant town to be based in. I had got to know Preston a little during the war years when I was in the forces and the idea of playing there was one I was happy about. After I left in the 1956-57 season, I played for Millwall and that was a terrible experience. It was a condition of my getting a benefit, but I only stayed 12 months. My wife wouldn't even go to the games it was that bad. I was relegated in my first year at Preston, but I thought we had some good players and everyone was confident we would be back."

At the White Bull at Bamber Bridge, near Preston, a sombre funeral service took place. A small coffin was loaded into a hearse and driven through the streets with the congregation silently filing behind as part of a ritual established years before. One of the pub regulars acted as clergyman and read a few well-chosen words for Preston North End Football Club, which had 'died and been laid to rest'. The coffin was lowered into the cellar of the pub, the entrance to which had been surrounded with artificial grass for the occasion.

Roland Jessop had received an invitation – the event had to be by invite only to keep out Blackburn Rovers fans who may not have appreciated the solemnity of the service – because he played for a local soccer team. He recalls: "People were genuinely moved. They were sick at the idea of North End in the Second Division. Football and what it meant to people was different then. After the service, everybody drowned their sorrows. The streets were packed for the procession and it was a tradition that even then had gone back years. The body of Preston North End would remain buried until the club were promoted again. Fortunately, it was not down there for too long."

Away From The Big Time

PRESTON had just two seasons in the Second Division before returning to the top flight where their loyal fans had no doubt they belonged. There had been hopes that they could bounce straight back in 1949-50, but such dreams were soon to evaporate in a largely disappointing season. However, the following year saw North End emerge as champions, clinching the title with a game to spare.

The two seasons in the lower division also saw a change in personnel as many of the players who had served North End so well during the Forties departed, while players who would be key components in North End's success over the coming few years arrived. Among the debutants were Willie Cunningham, Tommy Docherty, Willie Forbes, Eddie Quigley, Joe Marston and Charlie Wayman. The most notable departure was that of Bobby Langton.

Willie Cunningham didn't have long to wait before he got his chance in the first team. Preston were often big players in the transfer market and having paid £5,000 for his services they were keen to get value for their investment. It was to prove a shrewd buy as he quickly settled into the side and would play for North End in three decades after making his debut in the 1949-50 season.

He remembers: "Preston had been relegated before I arrived but a few new players had joined and we had the makings of a good side. I got my chance in the second game of the season, against Grimsby Town, and to me it was just another day. There were no nerves. I'd played a lot of games in Scotland and although the standard in the Second Division was higher than I was used to, I coped all right and was quite confident in my ability. We had a good defence, but goals were a bit of a problem and it takes a while for a side to get to know each other."

Another player who would make his debut later in the season and become a Deepdale legend was Tommy Docherty. His fellow Scot, Cunningham, says of him: "He was a bit of a rum one I can tell you. I'll say this of Tommy, I was glad I was playing with him rather than against him. Tackling was his strength and when he tackled them they stayed tackled. When we won promotion, he was a rock in defence."

Docherty was signed from Glasgow Celtic for £4,000 in November 1949 and was to be another shrewd capture. With fellow half-back Willie Forbes and Australian centre-half Joe Marston they formed a back line feared in the First Division and provided the defensive platform from which North End's bids for glory were launched in the early Fifties.

Military service had interrupted Docherty's playing days at Celtic and on his return from the Army he was happy to take up the chance to join North End and attempt to fill the considerable boots of Bill Shankly. Like his predecessor, his tough tackling and passion for the game quickly won the support of the home fans. Docherty was never a man to take a step back on the field, but although he is best remembered for those tackles, he had passing skills that are too often overlooked. It was late in the season before he got the chance in his favoured right-half position and was to make the shirt his own. He made 324 appearances for North End and won 25 Scotland caps. After being sold to Arsenal for £28,000 in August 1958, his last memory of North End was to be a painful one as he suffered a broken leg playing against his old club in a League game at Highbury. Like Shankly he is remembered as much as a manager as a player and was involved with Chelsea, Rotherham United, Queen's

Park Rangers, Aston Villa, Derby County, Porto, Scotland and his most famous club appointment as manager of Manchester United. He even had a spell as manager at North End.

Of Docherty, Tom Finney says: "I was very close to him in those days and he did not know the meaning of defeat. He was very much like Bill Shankly, the player he replaced in the Preston team, and it was obvious to me that he would follow Bill into football management just as he followed him in captaining the Scottish national side. Doc used to talk football night and day and he is just the same now. He had an infectious enthusiasm for the game and a tremendous sense of humour."

He remembers the trainer, Jimmy Milne, who would later manage the side, would often shout abuse at Doc and really criticise him. The player would slip into a temper and shout back, but he would still take the criticism on board and make sure he did not make the same mistake again. Any criticism made him more determined to succeed and his attitude was the right one for the club. Finney believes he was a truly great player and an important member of a very fine side and there was a terrific atmosphere in the dressing-room when he was there.

Joe Dunn recalls that Docherty was always the comedian in the dressing-room and helped create a good atmosphere. Willie Cunningham had bow legs so the Doc christened him 'Cowboy'. All the jokes were taken in good part. "On the field, though, it was a different story. Doc was a hard player and he would kick his auntie if she had the ball. He played fair but hard. He could only play one way and even in practice matches he just had to win the ball. He was a terrific lad."

As Walter Horan relates, Docherty was also one of the stars of the day who was aware that with large crowds bringing in lucrative receipts the players were getting a poor deal. Tom Finney was paid the same wage throughout the year while the rest of the squad had one wage when they were playing in winter and a lower summer wage. The Scot went to ask for the same treatment as Finney, only to be told by an unsympathetic official that he was not as good as Finney. "I'm as good as Tom Finney in the summer," was Docherty's response.

Docherty was always ready to help young players. Stuart Webb, who went on to become assistant secretary at Preston and then secretary, managing director and chairman of Derby County, recalls that when he was a youngster he wrote to Docherty asking for advice about becoming a good wing-half. "He wrote back telling me to train hard and practise a lot. He took the time to respond and I always remembered that. Funnily enough, years later our paths crossed on a professional basis when he managed Derby County."

As the 1949-50 season got under way, Preston fans had to get used to some unfamiliar visitors to Deepdale after the years of having top teams with star players performing before them. The likes of Chesterfield, Plymouth Argyle and Swansea Town hardly set the pulses racing, but there were still healthy attendances as the supporters rallied to the cause, sustained by the belief that the return of First Division football was not far away. There was also the chance to see Tom Finney in action, which was worth the admittance fee alone. Prices ranged from 1s 3d (8p) for the terraces up to six shillings (30p) for the best stand seats.

The campaign opened with an away defeat at Swansea and Preston's form on the road was to be disappointing with only six wins, which was never enough to make them promotion contenders. The new arrivals were beginning to gel, though, and the makings of a good team could be seen. An Easter double over local rivals Blackburn Rovers gave the supporters something to cheer and although sixth place was disappointing, things were starting to bode well for Preston.

Marian Bell remembers a trip to Chesterfield but it is not the match, which North End lost, which sticks in her memory. She has little recollection of the action on the field. What brings back vivid memories is the car she was travelling in breaking down. "It was cold for the time of year and the fan belt had gone. I remember I had to take off my tights so they could do an emergency repair and get us home. The sacrifices I made in following North End!"

Generally, she remembers fans being disappointed with life in the Second Division. "There wasn't the atmosphere and we missed not having the big-name teams at Deepdale. There wasn't the attraction to bring the fans and the crowds suffered. We were all convinced that this wasn't a division Preston should be playing in. We were to get plenty of practice in future years but for now we thought we were better than this."

One of her favourite players in the post-war years was Bobby Beattie, who was to remain at North End until 1953-54 season, although in his later years at Deepdale his first-team appearances were limited. Bell said: "He was the play-maker, a really skilful player who was never given the accolades and adulation his contribution deserved."

Beattie made his North End debut before the war, against Stoke City in October 1937, after moving south of the border from Kilmarnock for £2,250. He was a skilful player who enhanced Preston's reputation for playing quality, attractive football. The inside-forward was often the instigator of much that was best in the team's attacking play, creating glorious openings for his team-mates. He was a useful goalscorer himself, collecting 57 in his 264 League games for the club. He gained an FA Cup winners' medal in 1938 and a wartime Cup medal in 1941.

The Second Division championship-winning season did not start well for North End. There was only one win in the opening five fixtures and the form being shown did not look the stuff of title winners. Among the most disappointing games was the opening fixture of the season when the visitors were Manchester City, who had suffered relegation the previous season and were to return to the top flight as runners-up to Preston in this campaign. It was the Lilywhites who opened the scoring with a move started by Docherty with Quigley receiving the scoring pass from Anders. They were in front for only 30 seconds as City swiftly took advantage of a defence that had gone to sleep. Both sides had chances and perhaps later in the season, when both teams were again used to the pace of League football, they may have been taken. Shortly after the restart, Quigley was again on target, but as in the first half, City quickly replied with Dennis Westcott heading home a corner from John Oakes. Preston defenders were left vainly claiming offside while George Smith went on and scored to give the visitors the lead for the first time. Morrison hit the post with a shot that would have brought the equaliser, but the last word went to City with a goal for Clarke to bring a final score of 4-2.

On Christmas Day and Boxing Day, Preston played home and away fixtures against the same club, which was traditional. QPR were the opponents and the matches were to be memorable because they started a winning run for Preston, which established a record for both the club and the League. North End would notch up 14 League wins in succession, scoring 42 goals in the process with Barnsley the side to suffer the worst after being on the receiving end of a seven-goal drubbing at Deepdale.

Walter Horan remembers: "After we had won so convincingly at QPR on Christmas Day, 4-1, there was the return at Deepdale and it was a packed house with nearly 39,000 squeezed in. Everybody was expecting at least half a dozen and in our minds we had built the game up thinking it was going to be easy. Whether our players were over-confident or the Rangers side were more determined I don't know, but I remember we struggled. Angus Morrison got the only goal to win the points. The Christmas and Boxing Day fixtures were a great tradition and an important part of the festivities. Going to the football was as much a part of Christmas as turkey and plum pudding."

A revelation was centre-forward Charlie Wayman, who scored four at Loftus Road. Bishop Auckland-born Wayman, who began his career with Newcastle United, had been targeted by manager Will Scott after scoring a hat-trick against Preston the year before while playing for Southampton. He was just the established goalscorer the club needed. His first season produced a total haul of 27 and he was to prove a reliable scorer at the higher level as well. During the 1954 Cup run that would end at Wembley, he scored in every round. However, it was to be his last full season for the club as six games into the following season he was sold to Middlesbrough, to the consternation and anger of the home support, who failed to see the logic in manager Frank Hill's decision. Wayman averaged two goals in every three games for North End and finished his career at Deepdale with 117 goals in 171 League and Cup matches.

Horan recalls: "Charlie Wayman was a great player and for the fans the fact that we had signed such a high-profile goalscorer showed that the club meant business. All we wanted was to get out of the Second Division and back where we belonged. With Charlie knocking them in, that was going to be sooner rather than later. When he left I was shocked. It was unexpected and so pointless. It also showed how cavalier clubs could be with players in those days. Charlie had been a good servant to the club and produced some outstanding performances. He was loved by the fans. Yet they let him go. He was in the dressing-room and somebody came in and said he was wanted in the office. They just told him straight that he was going to Middlesbrough. He didn't want to go. I heard he wanted to play one more season for Preston and then finish."

The arrival of Wayman marked the departure of Eddie Brown, who went to Southampton as part of the deal. Brown remembers arriving in the south coast town and wondering how he would follow in the footsteps of Wayman, who had become a legend at The Dell. "I enjoyed Southampton immensely. There were not the traditions, the passion of the crowd or the quality of players that there had been at Deepdale, but for me I suppose I enjoyed being a bigger fish in a smaller pond. I also arrived on the back of the Wayman transfer and had been playing for a famous club like Preston, so I went straight into the first team." His career would see him go to Coventry City, Birmingham City, where he appeared in the 1956 Cup Final against Manchester City and Leyton Orient before finishing as player manager with Scarborough.

He added: "In a way I was glad to go. I wasn't a regular first choice at Preston and although I could have stayed, I was glad to be given the chance of first-team football. I enjoyed my time at Preston and I learnt a lot. I remember the chairman, J. R. Taylor, sitting across from me at a huge, highly-polished mahogany table and telling me when I signed for North End as a professional that the move I was making was very serious, very important and not to be taken lightly. He was right. Football means so much to so many people, especially in a town like Preston, which is a hotbed of soccer, that being a professional player cannot be taken lightly."

He added: "Although the money was never great, we were still on more than the average man in the street. If I had the chance to play my career again for the same wage, I would willingly do it just for the thrill and enjoyment of being able to run around at a fast pace and kick a football about in front of a huge crowd cheering you on. When you are out there, the money doesn't enter into it at all. I'll always be grateful to Preston North End for giving me my chance in football and letting me serve a valuable apprenticeship there."

Wayman made his debut against Birmingham City at St Andrew's on September 9. The home side went ahead with a goal inside five minutes when Johnny Berry (whose career was to be ended by injuries received in the Munich air crash) received the ball from a throw-in, his centre was not caught by goalkeeper Newlands and Bill Smith's header proved the only goal of the match. The finger of blame for the goal was pointed at the hapless figure of Newlands. Birmingham relied heavily on 'route-one' football while Preston were the more cultured side, but the home defence held out. Wayman had laid on some good passes, but colleagues had failed to profit from them. The centre-forward had few real chances at goal himself, but that was to come later. Among his tally was a hat-trick at Grimsby Town. He also got a brace in a 3-2 win against Southampton that was Eddie Brown's first visit back to Deepdale. Brown recalls that he was disappointed that he couldn't help his new club snatch at least a point, but there were no hard feelings and he enjoyed meeting up with old friends.

The Second Division championship was secured with Preston's 26th win of the season, at home to Hull City. A crowd of 37,827 saw a crisply-taken goal by Finney secure the points, although with North End by far the better side the winning margin should have been greater. With Hull's defence under siege for large spells in the game, Quigley in particular was unlucky to fail to get on the scoresheet. He was in the starting line-up because Wayman had failed to recover from a cold and withdrew on the day of the match.

Marian Bell remembers being at the game, but that there was not the excitement there was in the 1999-2000 season when Preston again won the Second Division title, even though this now equates only to the old Third Division. In 1951 it meant a return to the top flight of English football, but she said: "I don't remember the atmosphere being as electric in the Fifties for that match. I think everybody assumed that North End would go up sooner rather than later and we just accepted it as inevitable. Everybody was glad, of course, but it shows how the supporters' ambitions have changed over the years. The recent promotion has come after years in the wilderness, which is what made it so special."

Walter Horan remembers the growing excitement as Preston blazed a trail through the fixture lists. He was there to cheer them on and has memories of some wonderful moments: the four goals against QPR scored by Wayman; being two goals down against Leicester City and then some Finney magic turning the game around and Wayman again profiting with a brace of goals; a goal by Finney in a 4-2 win over Brentford in a match played on a mud bath in which the Preston man beat five players to score; and a winning goal against Hull City in the penultimate match of the season when he again waltzed around defenders before scoring and, in these days before histrionic goal celebrations, calmly walked back to the centre-circle as team-mates politely clapped.

With the title won, the final game against Doncaster Rovers should have been the chance to relax and treat their travelling support to an exhibition display. Yet it was not to be and the performance had echoes more of the opening match against Manchester City than the marvellous football produced for much of the second half of the season in that incredible winning run. The Yorkshire side's first goal fell to Ray Harrison after Gooch had saved a penalty-kick but the punched clearance fell too invitingly to the Doncaster player. The second was scored by Bert Tindill eight minutes from time. Doncaster's roughhouse tactics and reliance on brute strength knocked Preston out of their stride. They could at least reflect, though, that from August they would be meeting First Division sides that relied more on skill.

Preston had collected 57 League points and won the title by five points from Manchester City. It was the first time a championship shield had been at Deepdale since 1913 and marked the most successful season since the Cup-winning year of 1938. The manager Will Scott and the players were guests of the Mayor at a civic reception to mark the title win. A souvenir brochure was also produced to celebrate the triumphs of the season. To round off the football year, the team travelled to Switzerland for an end-of-season tour that combined a holiday with three games.

Finney remembers: "We had won the championship comfortably and a number of new players had arrived and enhanced the side, but what I was most pleased about was that we had earned a reputation as a really good footballing side. It was one of the best teams I was to play in at Preston, as the results in the First Division would show. I used to read in the newspapers about Preston being a one-man team and that everything was down to me, but that was rubbish when you consider the outstanding players we had."

Back To The Top Flight

PRESTON'S return to the First Division was not a case of struggling to bridge any sort of gap in class, but rather a demonstration that a squad which contained some key new faces from the one relegated two years before was more than able to hold its own at the higher level. There was, of course, still the presence of Tom Finney to put a stamp of genius on proceedings. He was now surrounded by players who could take on a share of the workload. As he himself says, football is a team game and no individual can achieve success on his own.

Players like Willie Cunningham, Tommy Docherty, Charlie Wayman, Joe Marston and Angus Morrison had emerged as quality performers who would revel at the higher level. They would have walked into the first teams of any of Preston's First Division rivals. At Deepdale they would take the club to within touching distance of the pinnacle of the game in both the League and the Cup.

A seventh-place finish in 1951-52 showed that the new arrivals to the top flight were comfortable at the higher level and gave an inkling of what was to come the following season when North End would mount their bid for the championship title, only to be so cruelly denied. For now, though, the fans could welcome back premier teams and a brand of football they had been denied for two seasons. And there were some wonderful displays for them to cherish. Not least two wins over keen rivals Blackpool in September with the Deepdale game played before a crowd of 40,809.

The squad was strengthened with Joe Dunn joining, although it would be a few seasons before he because a first-team regular. Another recruit was Bobby Foster and again, although he was not always an automatic choice, his presence in the squad meant there was talent to be tapped into if injuries or loss of form forced a change of line-up. He was also a versatile player who could play in various forward positions. He scored 42 goals in 110 League appearances for the club before being sold to Second Division Rotherham United in the 1956-57 season.

Twelve draws in the season was already starting to look like League points lost rather than gained, and at the finish Preston were 11 points behind champions Manchester United. A highlight was a trip to play at Old Trafford early in the season. United were in the lead through John Aston after only three minutes, but then found themselves up against a Preston side determined to limit their opportunities as defenders constantly harried the Manchester forwards, while at the other end the North End attackers showed they could match their more illustrious opponents in both skill and tenacity. United stars like Stan Pearson, Johnny Carey and Aston found themselves mastered by the likes of Cunningham, Morrison and Marston. The maestro himself, Finney, had a quiet game by his standards yet still created the opening for Wayman to score. For such a proven matchwinner, such glimpses of his best were all that were needed to turn a game. The winner was a shot from Quigley, who could easily have had a second. Preston dominated much of the first half and virtually all the second, such was the control they managed to exert. How the fans must have wished for a few more gilt-edged performances like this.

For the goalscorer Eddie Quigley, this was to be his last season at Deepdale. The player had established a British transfer record when he joined Preston from Sheffield Wednesday for £26,500 in December 1949. He had been at Hillsborough for two years after joining the Owls from Bury for £12,000 in October 1947.

Unlike many of Preston's rivals in East Lancashire, like Burnley and Bolton Wanderers, where the directors were unwilling to dip so deeply into the transfer market, at Preston they were brave enough to back their judgments with hard cash and saw buying players as a way of keeping Preston near the top of the professional game and their supporters happy. Indeed, it was only the day before Quigley signed on the dotted line that the club had paid £18,000 for Willie Forbes. It could be said that with Quigley, the gamble didn't pay off. After only 52 League games and midway through the season, he was sold to Blackburn Rovers for £23,500, less than Preston had paid for his signature. He did, though, manage 17 goals in that time. At Blackburn he enjoyed a fine career as a player and later managed the club.

Forbes, of course, represented much better value and his towering presence helped keep Dunn on the sidelines. He had joined from Wolverhampton Wanderers and was to spend six years at the club. He was another fiery Scot in the Preston ranks at a time when there were a lot of hard players in the League, although in those days before the proliferation of red and yellow cards it took something near to murder to incur the referee's wrath. In these times the violence was left to the players to sort out on the pitch. The supporters were civilised even if the professionals weren't. In fairness to Forbes, though, every team had what is euphemistically called 'hard men' and Preston were no exception. There was no quarter asked and none given.

Forbes was a man upon whom the team could rely when the pressure was on and he could get through a prodigious workload. He remained at Preston until 1956 when he moved to Carlisle United. He had played 191 League games for the Lilywhites and when his football career ended, he returned to the town.

Tom Finney puts into context the transfer fees, saying they were peanuts compared to today, even allowing for inflation. Yet other East Lancashire clubs, notably Bolton Wanderers and Burnley, were reluctant to spend. Bolton would win the 1958 FA Cup with their manager Bill Ridding proudly boasting that the side had cost only £110, which represented 11 signing-on fees of £10 each. Bob Lord, the autocratic chairman at Burnley, was another reluctant to dip into the coffers to secure talented players, preferring to rely on those coming through the youth set-up or plucked by scouts from local League football. The failure to buy was a source of resentment to the fans of these clubs. It says much for Preston that they were prepared to compete with the larger clubs and break transfer records. Finney does point out that the club was also in the vanguard of starting a youth policy to attract local lads and then nurture them through to first-team football. Indeed, Finney himself arrived as a 15-year-old in 1937.

Even at Preston, though, there was a tight control of the purse strings. Finney explained: "The finances in football clubs were generally solvent, unlike today. Nowadays there are only a handful of clubs that make money. In the Fifties, transfer fees were peanuts and the maximum wage kept a cap on the wage bill. Money was generated through the turnstiles and all the leading clubs did well. We averaged between 25,000 to 30,000 a game in the season and that meant the club was in pretty good financial shape. Once a player had signed for a club, he was virtually tied for life. There was no dictating terms. The club held all the aces."

In these times the directors took a much greater say in the sort of on-the-field matters that modern managers would not allow them to become involved in. It was not just in the buying and selling of players where they held sway. At many clubs they also had the last word on team selection and were not averse to giving advice on tactics, however unqualified they might be. Tommy Banks, the Bolton Wanderers and England full-back, recalls a director giving advice on marking the opposite winger. This was from a man whose football experience didn't extend beyond Sunday afternoon soccer.

He sums up his view of the directors of the day with an anecdote involving a game between Bolton and North End at Deepdale. "We were being played off the park and Tom Finney was at his best and by half-time we were losing heavily. A note arrived from one of our directors praising the side's performance. We were in our change shirts and he thought the team in white were us and not North End. That's a measure of what he knew."

Preston and Burnley fans were given something to talk about after their Christmas Day meeting and it had nothing to do with festive spirit or seasonal greetings. Burnley fan Harold Gee remembers the match produced a nasty confrontation between England and Burnley's Billy Elliott and Scottish international Willie Cunningham. "They were knocking hell out of each other for the whole game. At one point Cunningham was carried off on a stretcher and received treatment off the pitch, but then he shrugged off the arm of the trainer and ran back on the pitch and straight to Elliott. The other players had to stop him having a go. He wouldn't leave the field and Tom Finney, as captain, took the decision to move him to outside-right, as far away from Elliott as possible. That cooled things off, but there was expected to be a return encounter the following day when Burnley played North End at Deepdale. In the event, though, the match was called off because of fog."

Fifty years on, Cunningham still remembers the incident and it provokes a strong response. "Don't talk to me about Elliott. He was a dirty bugger who kicked anything that moved." Gee has some sympathy with the ex-North Ender. He recalls: "Elliott was a niggly player. I had friends who were drinking in a pub where Elliott was drinking on his own. They recognised him because they were Burnley fans. Elliott called them over and said: 'If you've anything to say, say it to my face. Now piss off.' They hadn't been calling him, but were just remarking that he was a Burnley player. Being sociable wasn't a strong point for Billy."

Tom Finney remembers the incident and that such bad blood was unusual in the Lancashire derbies in those days. Although they were hard games, tempers rarely flared to such an extent. He recalls: "There had been a few things going on between the two during the game and I remember it finally came to a head when Elliott took a throw-in and as the ball was played back to him, Willie Cunningham went into him and carted player and ball over the line. The referee was going to send Willie off and I was saying things to him like: 'You can't send him off on Christmas Day,' and he relented after I promised to switch Willie to the other side of the field. It was an uncharacteristic situation and Willie was usually level-headed, but there had been a few things going on and he lost his rag. What more usually happened was we had some cracking games with Burnley over the Christmas period."

Indeed, it is a measure of the camaraderie between the players in the East Lancashire clubs that after his retirement in 1960, Finney used to turn out in charity matches as a guest of the Ex-Clarets team. He has happy memories of the games saying: "Burnley were one of the first clubs to have an ex-players side and they raised a lot of money for good causes. They were well supported and because I knew all the Burnley players I was happy to turn out as a guest. It was a few years later before Preston established a similar team. We might have all been retired, but there was still a lot of people turned out to see us."

Charity games were to come later. For now there was the more pressing matter of League points and Cup wins. For Preston, the low point of the season came in the FA Cup. The team stayed at the resort of Weston-Super-Mare before the third-round tie against Bristol Rovers. The Eastville ground was infamous for its cloying mud, but trainer Jimmy Milne expressed his confidence that North End could cope with such conditions. Others, though, feared that Preston's intricate passing game and determination to play stylish football could be their undoing unless they were prepared to adapt their play to the conditions, which could only be a great leveller.

Prior to the game on January 12, North End had suffered two reverses on waterlogged pitches, losing away to Newcastle United and suffering a home derby defeat against Burnley. Letters to the *Lancashire Evening Post* urged the team to tailor their playing style to the conditions. A more direct approach might not please the aficionados of fine football, but was more likely to produce the desired result. Such entreaties fell on deaf ears. Bristol Rovers were a Third Division side and North End, not surprisingly, were short-priced favourites. The stage was set for one of those Cup shocks that are embarrassing to the pedigree side, a bitter blow to their fans, but yet to the neutral is what helps make the tournament so special.

Preston were already acquiring the tag of being a one-man team, and without the great man for this Cup-tie there was the chance to scotch the view that North End couldn't perform without Tom Finney. It was a chance destined not to be taken as Rovers ran out 2-0 winners. As had been feared in some quarters, Preston fell victim as much to the mud as the opposition players. Bristol raised their game and played with determination and great passion. They refused to be overawed or overwhelmed by their higher division opposition and took their chances well. Preston's players needed only to look at the footprints in the greyhound track that runs around the pitch to see what they faced; the footprints were ankle-deep. The Eastville pitch more than lived up to its reputation and it was an inglorious exit at the first hurdle for North End.

At their best, North End proved they were the better of any team in the land. When they hit form they could achieve impressive wins. In one three-game spell in November they scored 13 goals. Sunderland and Wolves both had four put past them and then when Huddersfield Town visited Deepdale the crowd were treated to five, with every forward getting on the scoresheet. Unfortunately, such good work was undermined with three draws and a defeat in the next four games. Still Preston ended the season on a high when they entertained Liverpool. They saved the best for last, producing their biggest win of the season with a 4-0 victory and if Liverpool were unlucky not to score then a resounding win was nothing less than Preston deserved. The forwards worked hard for each other and their speed of thought and movement was too much for the Liverpool defenders to cope with. Again the goals were spread with Wayman collecting two and one each for Morrison and Finney, the latter converting a penalty-kick.

Billy Scott recalls there was a good squad and competition for first-team places was tough. During the early Fifties, he faced a tussle for the full-back position with former Manchester United defender Joe Walton. An injury or a poor game could mean a spell in the Reserves. It was, though, a measure of the strength of the Preston team at this time and while sometimes frustrating, Scott was professional enough to accept the change in fortunes.

Joe Walton had been bought from United in 1948. His family recall that on the journey to the town the Reds' manager, Matt Busby, had a change of heart and tried to persuade the player to stay at Old Trafford. With the deal agreed and Walton convinced the change would be a fillip to his career, he resisted the plea. It was to be North End's good fortune that he did. He made over 400 appearances for the team and appeared in the 1954 FA Cup Final at the expense of Scott. He left in the relegation season of 1960-61 when he joined Accrington Stanley, but his spell there was short-lived and he played only 18 games for the Peel Park club.

During this period, Jim Proctor was a youngster being taken to the football for the first time by his father and he can remember the sense of excitement and the feeling that this was a special occasion when he visited Deepdale. The crowds seemed huge and he was passed over the heads of those packed on the terraces and sat on benches at the side of the ground, next to the policemen.

He said: "I can remember the characters in the crowd and the things they shouted. It was nothing obscene, just support for the team or some wisecrack. I remember on a pouring day at Burnden Park against Bolton Wanderers and an old chap was shouting his support for the home goalscorer, whoever it was. Suddenly his false teeth flew out and landed on the cinder track that ran around the pitch. Somebody gave them back and he just put them in his mouth and started shouting again. They must have been covered in cinders. For home matches we used to walk the six miles from our home in Bamber Bridge to the ground. Football was an important part of everybody's lives."

The first season back in the First Division was complete. It had been part of a year of consolidation. When things had started to go wrong with an 11-game run without a win in mid-season, the side had the strength of character to battle back. The average attendance was nearly 33,000 as the crowds flocked to support the side and they were regally entertained for their trouble. Now the stage was set for Proud Preston to make a bid for the biggest prize of all.

So Near, Yet So Far

IT WAS the season when Preston North End came close to fulfilling their dream and lifting the Football League championship trophy that their football in general and Tom Finney in particular richly deserved. In the end, goal-average was to see them deprived of the silverware as the honours went to Arsenal. It had, though, been a season that had captivated the town and held supporters enthralled. 'If only' were again the words on everyone's lips. Not since the 1889-90 season, when the club won the title, had they been so close to glory.

Yet the season had begun badly with only four wins in the first 15 games. There was nothing yet to give an inkling of the drama that was to come. However, it was quickly becoming clear that this side of the early Fifties was now reaching its peak. Not just Finney, but a whole array of players were all at the top of their game. The team also had a settled look and Finney was not troubled with injuries.

However, devoted fan Marian Bell for one did not believe North End would win the League and she was surprised that they finished as well as they did. In her view the team's great strength was also its weakness. The over-reliance on Tom Finney and the one-man-team nature of the side meant, she thought, that Preston would never produce the consistency of results that was needed for a title win.

She said: "With North End it was Finney or nothing. The other leading teams of the day had a greater balance and I think one of the reasons those in charge didn't invest in strengthening the squad to a greater extent was because they relied on Tom to carry the side. One or two new players could have made the difference between winning the League or Cup or falling just short, which is what happened. It was a blinkered outlook. I don't think we were really good enough to win the title, although we did come close and one result could have made all the difference."

A cherished memory for her is seeing Joe Dunn head the ball in heavy rain after a long clearance by the opposing goalkeeper and the ball burst as he made contact. She can still recall the shock on the player's face as all the water that had collected on the ball poured out and the sound was like a gunshot.

A new arrival in the forward line was Jimmy Baxter, cousin of Willie Cunningham. Baxter was signed from Barnsley as a replacement for Bobby Beattie. Although small in stature, he was a tough character who could bounce back from hard challenges and not be knocked out of his stride. He quickly fitted into the forward line with Tom Finney and Charlie Wayman and helped enhance Preston's reputation as a good footballing side. He played for North End for seven seasons, making 245 League and 22 Cup appearances and scoring 71 goals in total.

The most disappointing result in that early-season slump in form came with the visit of Manchester United. Then as now, the Manchester club had huge support that generated plentiful receipts, enabling Matt Busby to buy talent. Just as it is today, they were the team that all the rival Lancashire clubs loved to beat. The only difference in the early Fifties is that North End were often more than a match for them. However, on October 18, the Preston fans could barely believe what was unfolding before their eyes. The game was effectively over in the first 20 minutes as the Preston defenders were caught cold by a United side committed to all-out attack.

An error handed United their first goal after four minutes. Goalkeeper Newlands came out for a cross, but was left in no-man's land as Pearson arrived before him and headed into an empty net. Claims of offside fell on deaf ears and the visitors had the perfect start. It was to get worse for Preston, as with their confidence soaring the United forwards pressed forward and a 12th-minute goal was their reward when Aston seized on a parry by Newlands of a powerful shot by Jack Rowley. Two minutes later came another goal and again it was Aston the scorer, converting a cross by Johnny Berry. After 22 minutes Rowley saw his shot deflected on to the post by the 'keeper, only for the rebound to land invitingly for the forward and he made no mistake with his second chance. The first-half rout was still not complete with Pearson making it five. North End were to rally in the second half but the damage was done and the score remained 5-0.

The week before the United game there had been another heavy defeat when Preston travelled to London to face Chelsea and lost 5-3. Later in the season came the third and last time they lost by five goals and again it was Manchester United who inflicted the damage. The Old Trafford side finished only eighth in the League, but their performances against North End put a serious dent in Preston's title aspirations. It was not just the points lost. Those heavy defeats would play a crucial part when the goals averages were worked out at the end of the season. However, for the players there was an unfortunate accident that underlined the precarious nature of their trade and put League points and goal-averages into perspective. In a game against Sheffield Wednesday there was an accident involving goalkeeper George Thompson and the Owls' prolific scorer, Derek Dooley. It would ultimately cost the Sheffield player his leg.

An unbeaten run of nine games was completed with an impressive win in the third round of the FA Cup against Wolves, 5-2, in which Charlie Wayman scored a hat-trick. The highlight for many of the fans, though, was a sterling win against their great rivals Blackpool when the Seasiders visited Deepdale. Preston have nearer Lancashire rivals, but none is as fierce as Blackpool. The rivalry is mutual and more than 5,000 Blackpool fans had made the journey for the game. What added a particular edge for those on the terraces during this period was that the encounters had the added sub-text of the great Finney or Matthews debate as to who was the better. The supporters of both clubs had no doubt, each not surprisingly favouring their own man.

When Blackpool visited on January 1, Matthews was missing and his absence was to Preston's advantage. The scoreline finished 4-2, but that flattered the visitors. Preston dominated and went four goals up and it was only towards the end, when they eased off the pressure, that Blackpool were able to conjure two goals in the last 15 minutes to give some respectability to the result. Finney and Baxter orchestrated the attacking moves and Morrison profited with a brace and Wayman with one. A fourth goal fell to Finney himself. In defence, Marston excelled in keeping the great Stan Mortensen in check. Preston opened the scoring when a bad pass by Ernie Taylor was seized on by Baxter, whose pass fell to Wayman and he shot just wide of George Farm in the Blackpool goal. The second was a touch of Finney at his best as he dribbled the ball almost to the near post, where he drew Farm before sliding the ball to Morrison who had the simplest of tap-ins. With half-time approaching, two shots were cleared by defenders, but it was third time lucky for Preston when the ball rebounded to Morrison whose shot went through a mass of players. In the 68th minute, Finney scored when after appearing to be tackled and was able to athletically stretch out a foot and hook the ball wide of Farm. Late goals for Albert Hobson and Bill Perry took some of the gloss off the performance, but it was the North End fans celebrating at the end.

Having triumphed over Wolves in the third round of the FA Cup, Preston received no favours for the next round with more First Division opposition in the shape of Tottenham Hotspur. When Spurs had visited in the League, a Morrison goal had been enough to secure the points. This time, though, Spurs were able to hang on for a 2-2 draw that their determined defending deserved. A howling gale did not make for good football and was particularly unhelpful to Preston, whose neat football was best served by good conditions. Such was the interest the game had generated in the town that some fans were queuing outside the ground from 7.40am. Spurs opened the scoring and then again took the lead with goals that North End would have been disappointed to have conceded, particularly as the home side had the better of the play. A Finney penalty and a goal for Lewis ensured a replay, which the general consensus view felt was a fair result. Derek Lewis was a promising young player whose career was to be tragically cut short. To the shock of everyone at the club and in the town, he died following a brain haemorrhage in the summer of 1953. In the following October, a memorial match was played at Highbury against Arsenal with more than 25,000 attending.

As they arrived for the replay, the Preston players found the congestion was such that it was hard to get into the ground. Police on horses and on foot were trying to restore some order to the chaos and allowing people through a door in single file. By the time of the kick-off, there were 50,000 in the ground and many more still outside waiting to get in. A ninth-minute goal for Spurs was to decide the issue. Scott failed to clear and when 'keeper Thompson ran out to try to recover the situation, the ball was tapped away from him and Sonny Walters' shot took a deflection and lobbed into the net, just beating the despairing efforts of Cunningham to head it clear. If the goal had an element of luck about it, then it could not be argued that Spurs deserved their lead, being the most dangerous side on the park and creating by far the better chances. Finney found himself facing two or three men every time he got the ball, as Spurs' tactic was clearly to stop him at all costs. It proved an effective strategy, although Finney did have the chance to equalise with five minutes left when he finally slipped his markers and got his head to a centre from the left, only for the ball to hit the post from six yards out.

With the FA Cup a memory, North End could concentrate on the League and were to enjoy another epic encounter with Spurs at White Hart Lane in February, a little over two weeks after the FA Cup replay. Within eight minutes Spurs were 2-0 up and defeat was again staring Preston in the face. The fight back was not long in coming, though, with Finney scoring after 12 minutes and being at the centre of all that was best about Preston's play. Morrison looked to have brought the scores level when his shot beat the goalkeeper but was cleared off the line by a defender. To the visiting supporters' delight, it fell to the feet of Wayman who made no mistake. In the last minute before half-time, Len Duquemin scored twice to bring up his hat-trick and mean that in the second period the Lilywhites would again have to try to claw back a two-goal deficit. In the 55th minute, Wayman found the unmarked Morrison who shot into the far corner. Preston earned their hard-fought draw with a goal from Lewis in the 74th minute.

The Preston juggernaut gathered momentum as the season progressed. With four fixtures remaining, Preston faced three away matches and their only home game was against title rivals Arsenal. It looked a daunting challenge, but with the form the Preston side had been showing, anything was possible. The final run-in started badly with a 2-1 defeat by Charlton Athletic, but then Manchester City were beaten 2-0. Walter Horan remembers the town being gripped with excitement and fans praising the recent efforts, but wishing if only points hadn't been so easily squandered at the start of the season. Lost matches were recalled. So were draws that could have been wins. Everybody remembered a missed chance here or a careless slip there that had cost Preston dearly.

In the penultimate game, Arsenal were the visitors to Deepdale. A win for North End would take the title race to the wire and nearly 40,000 were crammed into the ground. In the view of many who witnessed the encounter, few could remember an Arsenal side being so totally outclassed. No neutral, unaware of what was at stake, would have identified the Gunners as a team that was going to win the title. The London side that was traditionally so secure in defence found themselves run ragged by a North End team that dominated for large periods of the game. A 2-0 win was comfortable, but it could have been so much better.

The Arsenal supporters released red and white balloons as their team appeared, but it was to be the only chance for celebrations for the Londoners. Both sides were nervous at the start, which was hardly surprising given what was at stake. A long kick by Cunningham was deflected and hit the post, but it was to be a temporary reprieve for Arsenal. Finney had cleverly beaten Leslie Smith and moved into the penalty area when he was brought down with a challenge from behind. Finney converted the spot-kick for his 16th goal of the season. Just before the break England international Smith was lucky not to concede a second penalty when he appeared to again foul Finney. This time North End's only reward was a corner. Smith, though, was being given a torrid time by Finney. A powerful shot by Wayman in the second half made the game safe. Goalscoring celebrations in the Fifties were normally fairly reserved, a handshake or a pat on the back generally sufficing. On this occasion, though, the centre-forward marked his goal by jumping into Morrison's arms.

The convincing win over Arsenal ensured that with each club having just one game to play, the championship was still undecided. Preston played on the Wednesday against Derby County, who were already doomed and at the foot of the table. There were no careless slip-ups as Preston collected the away win courtesy of a Finney penalty before a crowd of over 31,000 at the Baseball Ground.

The following Friday, Arsenal played host to Burnley, who had themselves enjoyed a good season and were to finish sixth in the table. It was fingers crossed in Preston that the East Lancashire side might do them a favour and ensure the title came north. Walter Horan remembers that the fans were hoping that a touch of brotherly love might hand North End the title.

He explained: "Having beaten Arsenal to keep our hopes alive, we felt we deserved the title. The Gunners had been completely outplayed. In goal for us was George Thompson and the Burnley 'keeper was his brother Des. Burnley were a good side and by all accounts it was a good game. There were more than 50,000 at Turf Moor and a good few had travelled down from Preston to lend their support."

In the end, though, it wasn't to be. Burnley started badly, but then rallied. However, it ended with the Gunners winning by the odd goal in a five-goal thriller. Arsenal were champions and for Preston it was a case of wondering what might have been. The team and Tom Finney certainly deserved something for their efforts.

Willie Cunningham recalls: "If you ask most professionals which they would rather win between the League and Cup, they will say the League. It is a better test of a team and you have to be consistent throughout the season. In the Cup you have to get a bit of luck on the day to go through. Usually in the League, the luck evens itself out over a season and at the end there is a clear winner. When the title is decided on goal-average, though, it is bitterly disappointing. You have come so close. Having beaten Arsenal so well towards the end of the season, nobody away from Highbury could have begrudged us our triumph. To have come so close and just to miss out was heartbreaking. A decimal point deprived us of a place in history."

The Road To Wembley

IF THE previous season had so nearly brought glory in the League, then the 1953-54 campaign, under a new manager, Scott Symon, was to see the FA Cup dominate the hearts and minds of the people of Preston. This was the year in which North End went to Wembley, where they met West Bromwich Albion. The previous year, Stanley Matthews had finally gained his Cup winners' medal at the third attempt in the epic Final against Bolton Wanderers. All hoped that this would be the year for Tom Finney to emulate his achievement and gain some domestic honour for his outstanding contribution to the game.

Finney's injury jinx again struck, keeping him out for half of what was ultimately a disappointing League season with Preston finishing 11th. He was there for the big showdown at Wembley, but it was to be a disappointing affair for the great player. North End lost 3-2 and Finney put in a moderate performance.

Looking back on his illustrious career he says of the Cup Final: "It was my most disappointing memory from my years in the game. It was a great occasion to get there and it's fair to say that it's every player's ambition to play in a Cup Final and get a winners' medal. There's everything for the winners and nothing for the losers. There was all the hype about Stan Matthews winning the season before, but Stan had been in three and lost two. We started as favourites, but it was not to be. I had a poor game and just couldn't seem to get into the match. I played against Len Millard in League matches and always did well against him, but on the day he had an outstanding game. We didn't play anywhere near as well as we should or could have done. Afterwards I just wanted the ground to open up and swallow me."

There was also to be disappointment for Bill Scott who, after a tussle for the number-three shirt with Joe Walton that had seen them share the position in previous seasons, was now to find age and injuries taking their toll. He went on a free transfer to non-League Wigan Athletic after suffering first a knee injury and then appendicitis.

He said: "It was disappointing to miss the chance to go to Wembley, but I enjoyed my time at Preston. It was my local club and that's always a bit special. The benefit North End gave me raised the money with which I bought the house I still live in. In football you get the good and bad times. Relegation and missing out on Wembley were the lows, but there were lots of highs. I've no regrets and I still see some of the players from that era."

Charlie Wayman was again the marksman in form, managing to score in every round in the FA Cup during a season in which he finished with a total of 32 League and Cup goals. He became the only player in the entire Football League to have scored 20 or more goals in each of the previous six seasons. A goal by the centre-forward and one for Finney were enough to account for Derby County (by now a struggling Second Division side) in the third round and then a trip to another Second Division club, Lincoln City, provided few problems as Preston again triumphed 2-0 with Baxter on this occasion joining Wayman (whose 100th goal for Preston it was) on the scoresheet. George Thompson saved a penalty. It earned North End a fifth-round tie against Ipswich Town, who that season would win the Third Division South title.

The East Anglian club brought 2,000 supporters to Preston for the tie and with both clubs sporting blue and white colours, the early invasion of Ipswich fans had people on their way to work wondering why North End followers were out so early. The view of the travelling fans was that their left-back Jim Feeney would be able to keep Finney in check. Ipswich were to be disappointed, although Finney was left with plenty of bumps and bruises to show for his troubles, many inflicted by Feeney. Still, a 6-1 score line was convincing enough and Finney got a goal with Wayman and Baxter each collecting two and Morrison bagging the sixth. The draw for the sixth round saw North End again take to the road, this time to face Leicester City, that season's Second Division champions. The draw seemed to pit the two clubs together with monotonous regularity. It was the fifth clash in 15 seasons and in 1934 they met at the same stage in the competition and it was City who triumphed to earn a place in the semi-finals after winning 1-0 at Deepdale. Four years later it was Preston who were the victors and in that year they went on to win the Cup. The hopes in the town were that history would repeat itself and that victory would see their side carry on to Wembley. Leicester, though, could also draw on the ties with their regular Cup foes as a happy portent for the future. In 1949, Leicester won 2-0 and went on to Wembley, although they were to lose to Wolves. That match had unhappy memories for Finney, who broke his jaw. In 1951, North End won 3-0 with seven players who would take the field in the latest tie, namely Wayman, Cunningham, Docherty, Forbes, Finney, and Morrison. North End were short-priced favourites to progress, although, as it turned out, it was to be a marathon encounter.

Leicester's home form in the League had been impressive leading up to the game, albeit against Second Division opposition. Still wins of such impressive margins as 9-2, 6-0, 5-0, 4-0, and 4-1 showed they were a team in form and one not to be taken lightly. They went into the game with seven successive victories to their credit and North End were in no doubt that this was a side that could not be underestimated. Certainly the 4,000 Preston fans who made the journey south, many wearing blue and white toppers, knew they faced a tough match, although all were confident of success. Preston had been allocated only 2,000 tickets, so half the fans knew they would have to begin queuing early or rely on buying from touts outside the ground.

All the predictions about the game came to pass, with Leicester striving hard through their forwards, but finding the Preston defenders in no mood to give an inch. The pace was fast and furious, the entertainment value was high, and for the visiting fans, a 1-1 draw was a satisfactory result ensuring a return at Deepdale. Some of the roughhouse tactics used to cope with Finney certainly incensed the visiting supporters, but the player himself was becoming used to being on the receiving end of such treatment, particularly against lower division opponents in the Cup. Morrison gave the Lilywhites the lead and Foster had the chance to make the game safe shortly after. In the end a defensive howler by Thompson in the 75th minute gave City the equaliser when the goalkeeper misjudged a 35-yard free-kick by Ron Jackson that went over his head into the goal.

If the Lancashire clubs Preston and Bolton Wanderers could come through their respective replays then it would set up a semi-final to savour. Bolton, having been at Wembley the previous season only to lose against Blackpool in the Matthews Final, faced a replay against Sheffield Wednesday. Preston had the task of overcoming Leicester, but now confidence was running high that it could be done and for the first time many of the players started to believe this could be their year for Wembley. In the other semi-final, the draw pitted West Bromwich Albion against Third Division North champions-elect Port Vale, who were only the second club from the Third Division ever to reach the last four (Millwall of the Southern Section being the others, before the war). Vale's win against Cup holders Blackpool in the previous round was one of the biggest shocks in the history of the competition.

There were plenty missing from work on the Wednesday of the replay as more than 38,000 people poured into Deepdale for the eagerly-awaited match. With trouble among opposing spectators still two decades away, the match was not made all-ticket and there was no need to segregate fans, so a huge contingent of Leicester supporters queued up with the Preston fans for the ground and paddocks.

Marian Bell was among the thousands who had gone straight from work. She knew it would be difficult to get into the ground, such was the interest in the town, and the crowd eventually numbered 38,130. However, she was one of the successful ones and took her place waiting for the kick-off.

She said: "We were packed in like sardines and I was waiting for my husband and kept saying to my mother that I didn't think he had made it inside. We were always at the same spot on the halfway line, but with such a big crowd I feared he had been locked out along with hundreds of others. Then I saw him emerge from the entrance for wheelchairs and invalids, walking as though he had a stiff leg. There was no chance of him getting in the ground any other way and he wasn't going to miss the game, so he cracked on to the people at the entrance that he was unable to walk properly. We used to joke about that for years afterwards."

The game itself opened with the teams closely matched with Finney giving the home side the edge, but it was Leicester who took the lead after a quarter of an hour when Peter Small seized on a poor clearance by Joe Marston and his shot gave Thompson no chance. Buoyed by this success, City began to take the initiative and had the better of the chances as the half progressed, but at the interval one goal separated the sides.

A stiff team talk at half-time saw Preston emerge more determined and within seven minutes the scores were level when Leicester were made to pay for a foul on Finney. Cunningham's free-kick found Morrison on the left who headed back across goal where Wayman's header found the net. Some neat passing between Rowley and Small split the Preston defence and it was Rowley who applied the coup de grace. It was left to Morrison to bring the scores level again. After extra-time failed to produce a goal, it was down to another replay. It had been edge-of-seats stuff for the home fans and there could have been few complaints if North End had bowed out at this stage.

The venue for the replay was Hillsborough, which gave Sheffield Wednesday a chance to cast an eye over their semi-final opponents after the Yorkshire side had accounted for Bolton Wanderers. There were fitness tests on the journey to Sheffield for Finney, Wayman and Forbes, but to the relief of the Preston fans all three were declared fit. After their tense battles in the previous rounds this was to be a more comfortable outing for Preston as they triumphed 3-1.

Early in the game there was a piece of play-acting by Arthur Rowley, common in today's Premiership but rare in the Fifties. After a tussle with Bobby Foster, he rolled over in agony, only to enjoy an amazing recovery within a minute. It fired passions among supporters of both sides. Baxter started and finished the opening goal for Preston when his pass found Morrison out on the wing. His cross was contested by Wayman and goalkeeper John Anderson and the ball was only partially cleared into the path of Baxter, whose volley was fired home. With nearly an hour gone, the lead was increased with an unusual shot by Foster who, from the by-line and just outside the penalty box, managed to send the ball over the goalkeeper's head and into the far top corner. Rowley got one back when, with the Preston players appealing for offside and the linesman's flag raised, the referee allowed the forward to carry on and score. With ten minutes left, any thoughts of another replay were laid to rest by a Finney header from a free-kick by Forbes. The three games between the sides were watched by a total of 122,421 spectators who paid more than £20,742, an average of 5s 6d a head (28p).

In this FA Cup campaign, Preston were now to face their first opposition from the top division. The setting for the semi-final against Sheffield Wednesday was Maine Road and it attracted a crowd of more than 75,000. The Preston allocation of 25,000 tickets was sent by taxi once the result of the replay was known, and crowds were quickly queuing waiting for the sale to begin. The *Lancashire Evening Post* received a flood of letters complaining about the way the tickets were distributed. The main problem, of course, was that demand outstripped supply and 4,000 with stand season tickets for Deepdale were guaranteed a ticket, yet there were only 2,000 Maine Road stand tickets made available to Preston fans. Applying for some of Manchester City's share was not an option as the club quickly sold out, such was the interest the match was generating. Many neutrals were keen to be there to see Tom Finney.

In Lancashire they would have loved the semi-final to have been a battle royal between Preston and Bolton Wanderers, but Sheffield

Wednesday proved the party-poopers to that idea and, although struggling in the League, they now provided tough opposition. The groundswell of opinion, though, was that this would be the season in which Finney at the height of his powers would parade his talents on the Wembley stage. Such a view in the town of Preston and beyond was to be fulfilled. If anything, the biggest threat in the run-up to the match was the fear of over-confidence, given Preston were such clear favourites. There was also the view that North End, being a good footballing side, would be happier against more skilful opponents rather than against sides in the lower division who would be keen to use muscle rather than finesse against the talented Preston players.

Wednesday had endured stuttering fortunes in their Cup campaign, drawing at home against neighbours Sheffield United only to win the replay, and being held by Third Division North club Chesterfield at home before again travelling for a replay and winning. Having defeated Everton, they drew with Wanderers at Hillsborough and then made the tricky journey to Burnden Park and emerged 2-0 winners. The feeling, though, was that Preston were good enough to beat any team.

League form at the beginning of the season, when the sides played each other twice, gave little clue. Preston had won convincingly 6-0 at Deepdale, but the Wednesday goalkeeper Dave MacIntosh was injured for much of the match. When the sides met two weeks later, it was the Yorkshire side who showed their class with a comfortable 4-2 win. The fans endlessly discussed the permutations. Wednesday's appalling defensive record – they were to concede 91 goals that season and only narrowly avoid relegation – must surely give opportunities for Preston's potent strike force? Finney at his sublime best must surely be irresistible? Wayman, a proven goalscorer against the best defences, should triumph against the Owls' leaky back line? Preston had been favourites before in semi-finals and lost, but surely this time they would come good, reasoned their fans.

Indeed, it was to be a virtuoso performance by Finney to delight the Preston following and ensure a place at Wembley. Wednesday were left bewildered by his skills and North End's presence in the

1954 FA Cup Final was undoubtedly the outcome the neutrals wanted. The result was never in doubt after the first ten minutes and Wednesday were left completely outplayed by their Lancashire rivals. McIntosh in the Sheffield goal won praise for keeping North End at bay in the first half, but barring a dramatic change in fortunes for his side, the outcome was never in doubt. Preston matched their opponents in determination and had far more talent. In defence Harry Mattinson had a good game standing in for the injured Cunningham. Finney was the orchestrater of both goals. First he threatened to dribble and then centred, giving Wayman the chance to profit, and then for the second he left defenders stranded before centring for Baxter to score with a powerful shot. With West Bromwich Albion overcoming Third Division Port Vale in a Staffordshire derby, the stage was set for the Final. Albion, chasing football's Holy Grail of the League and Cup double, and Preston North End, the team renown for their footballing skills.

Preston supporters were convinced this would be their year, not least because the side were playing well and, of course, had Finney in its ranks. Albion had failed in the League after vying with Wolves for much of the season. They finally lost out as results went against them and the double slipped from their grasp, although they finished as runners-up. Could they recover sufficient composure and restore morale in time for Wembley? Preston fans felt they could not and even in the West Midlands there was a view abroad that the confidence of the side had been dealt too big a blow by the faltering progress in the League championship race.

Marian Bell recalls the euphoria of the semi-final win and the excitement in Preston now that the team would be going to Wembley. Now came the not-inconsiderable task of trying to secure Cup Final tickets. She recalls: "I queued all night for a ticket. I had taken with me blankets, cushions and what have you, and I settled down with hundreds of others. Unfortunately, for all my efforts I only got one ticket. My husband had been working and couldn't join the queue, so we tossed a coin and I lost. I never spoke to him for a week afterwards."

She added that there was unhappiness in the town at the way the tickets were distributed. There seemed to be no proper system and those with the money to buy from touts got them. But how the touts came by them in the first place, and how people who rarely went to Deepdale now had precious tickets for Wembley while regular fans didn't, was something that was never properly explained.

She said: "All I know was that I was heartbroken having seen Preston get so far and then to miss out for the Final. My husband had just come out of the forces and, like many people, we hadn't the money to buy black market tickets on top of the cost of a trip to London. Along with the rest who were left behind, I had to follow the game on the radio. There was, though, a wonderful atmosphere in Preston. It was tremendous. The shop windows were all blue and white and the people not going to the match still wore their rosettes. It was Cup fever and it was marvellous. The football team had helped put Preston on the map."

In the run-up to the game, she joined thousands of other disappointed fans in following any rumour about possible tickets. "There was always talk that tickets were available. A friend of a friend had one spare, type of thing. Even though commonsense told you it was hopeless, you still followed every lead in the forlorn hope there might be a ticket at the end of it, but sadly for me there never was. My husband went the night before the game, on the train. I sat at home and sulked."

Her husband was one of the lucky 20,000 Preston fans who made the journey to Wembley to cheer on their side. With demand far outstripping supply, there were touts charging £4 for a 3s 6d (18p) ticket. Many travelled through the night and grabbed what sleep they could in the West End or at the railway station before making their way to Wembley. The players enjoyed a late breakfast at their Surrey retreat and were in confident mood.

Kathleen Morrison had enjoyed the trip to London with the other players' wives and they had been booked into the Savoy Hotel. The players themselves would join them after the match. As the kick-off approached she remembers getting nervous in case Angus did anything wrong or made a mistake. Such was the expectation of the whole town riding on the players' shoulders.

She said: "The Final build-up was nerve-wracking, but we were being treated like royalty which was marvellous. Afterwards everybody was disappointed, but there was a big party with Norman Wisdom doing the entertaining. On the Sunday everybody went on a tour of London."

Sightseeing tours were for later, though. The fans had arrived with confidence but it was not to survive the 90 minutes of Wembley action. Putting their recent League form behind them, West Brom won the game 3-2 and managed, in the process, to keep the great Tom Finney quiet. In the opening minutes there were two crunching tackles on Finney and he never was able to stamp his authority on the game. It was an anticlimax for those who believed he could turn the Cup Final Preston's way. He was later to win the Footballer of the Year award from the football writers, but it was a poor consolation. All that was left was for the North End players to promise they would come back the following year and on that occasion lift the Cup. It had happened when Preston were the losing Finalists in 1937. They hoped it would happen again. There was also the chance to enjoy the plaudits of the massive crowds who welcomed them back to their home town, despite not being able to show off the trophy.

Walter Horan was there and recalls: "We all expected Tom to win the Cup for us, along with the rest of the team of course! Afterwards Tom admitted his skills had deserted him that day plus West Brom knew where the danger would come from and knocked him about a bit. Another point that most people forget was that Stan Matthews' show against Bolton the previous year was his third bite at the cherry to Tom's one. The saddest part for me was when North End came down from the Royal Box and started to walk around the pitch when someone must have said: 'Let's get out of here lads,' and they all galloped off to the sanctuary of the tunnel. It brought home to me what an awful place Wembley must be for the losing Finalists. Surely the FA could come up with some sort of presentation so that they could leave with a real sense of dignity."

He had travelled down with a few friends and had got his ticket from one of the players he knew from his former days at the club. While he enjoyed the match, he was less keen on Wembley itself. He said: "It was quite an occasion but I felt a Cup Final should never be played there. I would rather it was somewhere like Old Trafford or Villa Park with a more natural atmosphere. Wembley wasn't as palatial as I thought it would be and it was very ordinary. It was also a rip-off. There were people there who had probably never been to a football match and they had brought their wives. Tickets went on the basis of who you knew rather than how keen a supporter you were. I know one player who received a dozen tickets and he gave them to a bookie he owed money to. It wasn't just Preston, there were complaints about the ticket distribution every year."

Joe Dunn had travelled down with the reserve players on the Saturday morning and remembers the view among the members of the squad watching the events on the field unfold was that Preston were not playing well. As befits a professional he wishes he could have been out there. Whether he would have made any difference is something nobody will ever know.

He said: "When you are watching from the side and things are not going well, you always think you could make a difference. Maybe it would have been worse. I'd played a few games early in the season, but was injured before the FA Cup rounds started and the team was playing well so I wasn't brought back. The atmosphere on the day was terrific and it is a great regret that I never got to play at Wembley. I would have loved to have done. During the build-up to the game, the whole town came alive. Afterwards everybody was down in the dumps."

Angus Morrison admits: "It was a tremendous feeling to run out on to the pitch and be hit by the wall of sound. I didn't think we would be beaten, but there you go. Tom Finney at his best was brilliant, but he wasn't at his best that day. It would have been good to win and have something to show for what was a very good team. I learned the game at Derby, but I spent the best years of my playing career at Preston."

Wilf Wareing watched the game on a small 12-inch screen television and the house was packed because TVs were still relatively rare and all the neighbours had crowded in to see the drama unfold. "The excitement in the house was brilliant as the teams came out of the tunnel, but as the game went on it was obvious some of our players were not playing to their potential and that included Tom Finney. In fact I think he probably had one of his worst games. When it was all over we were stunned. Nobody was talking. Words couldn't describe how we were feeling. Even watching on television, though, it had been a special occasion."

Marian Bell had listened to the game on the radio on her own and the disappointment surpassed the heartbreak of not getting a ticket. Her husband had returned straight after the match, such was his disappointment. The whole town could not believe the match had been lost. It was a bitter pill to swallow.

Willie Cunningham remembers the whole build-up to the game passing in a whirl from which, years on, it is hard to pick out the detail. "It is one of the highlights of any player's career and there was also the sense that this meant so much to everyone in the town. I tried to keep the build-up as low key in my mind as possible but it's hard. The Cup Final was all that everyone was talking about. Losing was a crushing blow, but I enjoyed the whole build-up. When I see the losing teams now after the match, I know exactly what they are going through. I've been there."

Fan Jim Proctor remembers watching the Final on television and everybody in the room being anxious for a Preston win, not just because they were fans but for Tom Finney. Even at a young age, he remembers the result was a real sickener and the feeling of disappointment amongst everybody. It had been Preston's big chance to collect a trophy and it had gone begging.

Yet Preston had their moments. After England forward Ronnie Allen had put Albion ahead after 20 minutes, Angus Morrison headed Preston level less than a minute later after Tommy Docherty had crossed the ball into the West Brom penalty area. Early in the second half, Finney at last shook off Millard, got the ball to Baxter and then Wayman kept up his record of having scored in every round of that season's competition when he put Preston ahead with a goal that looked suspiciously offside. Wayman took it well, but Albion's defenders were furious. Midway through the second half it was Preston's turn to complain when Docherty was harshly adjudged to have brought down Johnny Nicholls and Allen made it 2-2 from the penalty spot. Thompson touched the ball but could not prevent it from entering the net. Albion now looked the more likely winners and with three minutes remaining, George Thompson, so often a Preston hero, misjudged a cross-shot from Frank Griffin. The ball ran along the goal-line before bobbling into the net. West Brom had won the 1954 FA Cup Final. Preston were runners-up, Cup Final losers, and only too ready to seek refuge in their dressing-room.

It was also the last game in charge of Preston for manager Scott Symon. A few days after the Wembley defeat, Symon opened a letter from the Glasgow Rangers secretary, Jimmy Simpson. It was an invitation for Symon, a former Rangers half-back, to return to Ibrox as manager. He had made his name by shaping, with little resources at Methil, the best team that East Fife had ever enjoyed. That success had led Preston to appoint him and he had immediately taken them to a Cup Final. Now Rangers wanted him and, of course, he would return home.

Tom Finney rates Scott Symon as possibly the best manager he played under at Preston and, for certain, his departure shocked the playing staff at Deepdale. Symon, who had played both football and cricket for his country, was one of the most tactically aware managers in Britain, and a great motivator, a man who could get a team playing to their full potential week after week.

Sir Tom Finney

TOM Finney was a football genius whose talents helped take Preston North End to the very highest levels in the game in the Fifties and whose contribution to England's cause was immense. When the subject of England's greatest player is raised, other names will be put forward, but Finney has an irresistible case. Certainly in this era, only Stanley Matthews, of Blackpool and Stoke City, is talked of as a possible challenger to the title.

Finney won 76 caps for England, and at the time only Billy Wright had more. He scored 30 goals, a record on his retirement matched only by the great Nat Lofthouse of Bolton Wanderers. He played 442 League games for North End, a figure that would have been higher but for injuries, which blighted his career. When he hung up his boots in April 1960, it was said that English football could ill afford to lose a man of his stature.

The great secret of Finney's success was his versatility. He was the true all-round footballer. He could play outside-right, outside-left or centre-forward and was equally skilled in any of the positions. None of his rivals had such a utility role. It was a talent exploited by both England and North End.

It is impossible to guess the value a man of his brilliance would command were he playing nowadays, and those who played alongside or against him have no doubt that his skills would make him a world-beater in the modern game just as he was in his own playing era.

Yet despite being part of a great Preston North End side, Finney was never to enjoy League or FA Cup glory. There were no winners' medals for the great man. There was to be just 'if onlys' as during the Fifties the club came so close to achieving success, but failed at the final hurdles. Finney is disappointed, of course, but pragmatic.

He said: "I felt at the time that there were a number of outstanding teams in the First Division. Teams like Manchester United, Wolves, Arsenal and Spurs all had outstanding sides during the decade. Unlike the Premiership nowadays, where two or three sides at most have a chance, the League was much more competitive then. In the Cup you always need a bit of luck to go all the way. We did come close and we did it playing attractive football."

The man who served an apprenticeship as a plumber during his early football days, and later built a successful business in the town following his trade, also established for himself a reputation as a down-to-earth man far removed from the prima donnas of modern football. Even now on his weekly visits to the offices of the Preston club where he is president, there are the football strips and scarves waiting to be autographed. It is a task he undertakes willingly. Finney the man has won as much respect as Finney the player and that is no mean feat. His contribution to football was recognised in 1998 when he was awarded a knighthood in the New Year's Honours List.

Finney was playing for junior side Holmslack Juniors when he saw an advertisement in the local newspaper inviting interested youngsters to Deepdale for a trial. He replied but heard nothing from Preston, who might have missed out on their most talented star. However, Finney's father knew the trainer and had a word and within a few days a card was received inviting him for a trial.

He recalls: "There were about 30 youngsters there and we had 20 minutes each. Afterwards my father was approached by an official to see if I wanted to join the ground staff. I was already 15 months into my apprenticeship and there was no way my father would be persuaded to let me go. He said I needed to have a trade and I was bitterly disappointed. My father's view was that too many youngsters were taken on after trials and by 18 they were on the scrapheap. It was important that I had a trade and it was really sound advice. So many players had nothing when their careers were over. In later years I used to ask retiring players what they were going to do and they had never even given it a thought. Running a pub or sports shop or working as a sales rep was what many went into."

Finney originally made his debut for the club playing in a junior side at outside-right against Manchester United. He signed professional forms in January 1940. In 1941 he won a wartime Cup winners' medal in the Football League Cup Final in which Preston held Arsenal to a draw at Wembley before winning the replay 2-1 at Ewood Park. Facing the experienced defender Eddie Hapgood (no one won more England caps than Hapgood between the wars) the young Finney already showed he was a talent to be cultivated. In between training and playing, he was still working in the plumbing business. The player winning the adulation of supporters on the terraces on a Saturday could be the plumber unblocking the drains the following Monday afternoon.

During the war, Finney served in the Royal Armoured Corps and became a star of the Wanderers forces side in the Middle East, although he did not dodge active service and saw action with the Eighth Army during the Allies' push up the boot of Italy. Eventually, though, football took over again and the selectors, already taking note of his performances in wartime soccer, picked him for an unofficial international in Switzerland which the Swiss won 3-1. "Frankly," he said, "the Swiss were better prepared."

He made his full international debut for England against Northern Ireland in Belfast in September 1946. Finney had been in a squad of 14, but didn't expect to play, with Stanley Matthews being the automatic choice at outside-right. But Matthews was injured and the Preston man had his first cap.

He said: "Playing your first game for England is always a special occasion. I knew three or four days before the game that Stan was injured. I was 24 and just out of the forces and to be playing for England within a couple of months was wonderful."

Before a record crowd of 57,000 at Windsor Park, England won the first official Home International match since 1939, 7-2, and Finney marked his debut with a goal. Middlesbrough's Wilf Mannion, also making his full England debut, weighed in with a hat-trick. Two days later, at Dalymount Park, Dublin, Finney was in the first England team ever to play the Republic of Ireland. The Irish battled hard and it wasn't until nine minutes from time that the only goal of the game was scored. Mannion lashed in a shot, Shamrock Rovers goalkeeper Tommy Breen could only parry it, and Tom Finney was on hand to put the ball in the back of the net. It had been quite a satisfying weekend.

Tom Finney retained his place in the England side for games against Wales and Holland (which was won 8-2 with Finney again on the scoreshet). In February 1947, however, Preston lost 5-0 to a Stoke City side that contained Stan Matthews. It seemed to sway the selectors over the Matthews or Finney debate and when the England side to meet Scotland at Wembley in April was announced, the Stoke man had regained his place at Finney's expense. Finney returned for a friendly against France at Highbury and then both men went on the end-of-season trip to Switzerland and Portugal. Finney missed England's first post-war defeat, 1-0 in Zurich, instead playing in the 'B' international against the Swiss - a goalless draw - but Bobby Langton, the Blackburn Rovers outside-left, was injured and England coach Walter Winterbottom asked the Preston man, a natural left-footer, if he would play on the left wing in Lisbon.

The player's response was short and to the point: "I would play anywhere if England asked me." He had never played in the position before - although he had begun his career at inside-left - but the problem of how to accommodate both Finney and Matthews in the national side had just been resolved. England's visit to Lisbon was a hugely successful one - they won 10-0. What wouldn't England give today for the forward line that turned out that day: Stanley Matthews, Stan Mortensen, Tommy Lawton and Wilf Mannion were alongside Finney. Tommy Lawton and debutant Stanley Mortensen each scored four and Finney also got on the scoresheet with a cracker of a goal. Fittingly, Stan Matthews was England's other scorer, hitting the last of the afternoon.

Said Finney: "Before the game we were told that they were a world-class side and that the stadium itself was intimidating enough. But once Tommy Lawton opened the scoring, that was it. They even changed the ball to the lighter Continental type, but it made no difference."

He has many other memories, of course, but among the highlights were a 2-0 win against Scotland in front of 135,000 spectators at Hampden Park in April 1948, and a 3-1 victory in December 1954 over the reigning World champions West Germany at Wembley. The Germans had overturned the form book to beat the red-hot favourites Hungary, who had twice thrashed England.

When a football lesson was handed out by the Hungarians in a 6-3 win at Wembley in November 1953, Finney was on the sidelines and watched the game from the press box. "I was allowed to comment on the Hungarians, but I was not allowed to say anything about the England side. We weren't allowed to say very much at all. I just watched and thought they were brilliant. We had never seen a side play with a deep-lying centre-forward before and nobody was picking him up. He was feeding through balls and causing our defence all sorts of problems. I played in the return game in Budapest in May the following year, when we lost 7-1. We were given a real lesson, but I think it was taken on board and we came back pretty strongly.

There were other great moments, many shared with another England star of the Fifties, centre-forward Nat Lofthouse, who describes Finney as his favourite player he appeared alongside. He adds that he was, with George Best, the most complete footballer he ever saw. Lofthouse and Finney proved a devastating combination when playing for England. The two played in England teams together on more than 20 occasions and on 18 of them Finney laid on the goalscoring pass. Lofthouse said: "I don't think you can compare football of my era and today. There are too many variations in formations, tactics and players. I will say, though, that players like Tom and Stan Matthews would be good players today."

The two certainly made his job easier. "I was lucky enough to have had Matthews and Finney on the wings in my England days. All we needed to do was give it to those two and they would get to the by-line and get the ball over, lace facing away, and I would have a good chance of getting to it with my head."

Finney's Preston team-mate Willie Cunningham has no doubts as to his ability. "What was special about Preston North End was a fellow called Tom Finney. There were some good players at the club, some were internationals, but he was in a class on his own. He is the best player I have ever seen in my life. He had all the skills. He was brilliant when he was on that ball. He could mesmerise opponents with his skill. He was what made the difference at Preston. He used to make so much time for himself, I'm sure he could have taken a tea break if he had wanted to. Without Tom Finney, Preston wouldn't have survived as long as they did in the First Division."

Jimmy McIlroy was the star of a Burnley side that were to win the League title in the 1959-60 season and were a dominant force towards the end of the Fifties and the dawn of the Sixties. During his long career with both Burnley and Northern Ireland, he played against Finney on many occasions and has the utmost respect for the player and the man. Indeed, he revealed that when plagued by a persistent groin injury that threatened to blight his championship-winning season, Finney was one of the players he turned to for advice. The Preston man had plenty of experience of having his appearances curtailed by injury.

McIlroy says: "Tom Finney was the greatest all-round player I have ever seen. He could have played in any position on the field except perhaps goalkeeper. The man, in my book, was a genius and he had more all-round skills than I have ever seen in any other player. Among his many qualities were courage and determination."

He remembers a fortnight before Finney's own testimonial, the two were playing in a testimonial for Bob Paisley of Liverpool. Finney was so determined to score that he went for a 50-50 ball with the goalkeeper. Although most players wouldn't have bothered in a friendly match, he did because he was an honest and committed player. He sustained an ankle injury. Although two weeks later he wasn't really fit to play, he still went out there so as not to let his own fans down.

McIlroy adds: "I remember one night at Deepdale and Leicester City were the visitors and the ground was packed. What I recall most was that every time the ball went to Finney, the noise of the crowd receded in anticipation. There was almost silence and as he collected the ball, with every stride he made the volume went up as though somebody was turning a knob. It kept rising and rising. The atmosphere was sheer magic. By the time he released the ball, the noise had reached a crescendo. That night I don't think he disappointed the fans once when he got the ball."

He highlights Finney's speed off the mark, his raids down the wing, the mazy dribble allied to the accuracy of his crosses and shots, as skills that made Finney such a formidable opponent. "On the days when everything clicked he was the greatest player in the world. I don't remember any other playing making an impact on me like he did that night against Leicester."

Ray Charnley was a prolific centre-forward for Blackpool during the late Fifties and into the Sixties, but his memories of Finney go back further, to the days when he was a youngster and caught the Ribble bus to Preston from his home in Lancaster to watch his favourite team and its leading player. Later in his career, he was selected for an FA tour to Australia and the Far East that was managed by Tom Finney and he had the chance to fulfil an ambition and play alongside him as the now-retired legend still took part in a few games.

Charnley, who had a spell with Preston towards the end of his career, remembers: "We had a 90-minute bus journey to Preston when I was a lad and we knew that if we didn't get to the ground by 2.15, we wouldn't get in and that was largely because of Tom Finney. He was a great player and a terrific fellow. What you see is what you get with Tom. As a schoolboy, every game he played in seemed to be special. He was that outstanding a player."

Having played alongside both Finney on the FA tour and, of course, Stanley Matthews in his Blackpool days, the age-old debate of who was the best naturally surfaces. Charnley's view? "I don't think there was a great deal between then. Both were really nice people and both were great players. I was a little bit in favour of Tom because he scored a lot of goals and Stan didn't, but Stan used to make a lot. What I can say is that it is fantastic to have been able to play alongside both of them."

Finney was, of course, a one-club man. He has no regrets about that today, but such was the power which clubs held over players that he had little choice in the matter during his playing days. There was, in fact, an offer made from an Italian club, Palermo, after England had played Italy in Florence and Finney had produced an outstanding display.

He takes up the story: "After the game I was approached by the president of Palermo to see if I was interested in moving. I was on £14 a week at Preston and he offered me £120 a week, bonuses, and a £10,000 signing-on fee plus a car and a villa. Of course I was interested, but I warned him things work differently in English football. As I suspected, it never went any further. I put my case to the board and I was told simply: 'If thou doesn't play for us, thou doesn't play for anybody.' At the time it was very exciting and a great temptation. The board ensured it never got off the ground, but it would have meant uprooting and I had a young family and all my friends and was building the business. I have no regrets that it didn't happen."

To the fans, of course, he has always been special. In the club museum there is a picture of Finney with Bill Jessop that was donated by Roland. It features the two as lads when they travelled to a game in East Ham, London, as members of the Preston Boys' team and was a treasured memento in the Jessop family. Finney gave Roland and his wife Joyce a tour of the club before the presentation and then posed for pictures with them. He said: "Finney is a fantastic fellow and a real gentleman."

His skills on the field have been well-documented and Jessop concurs that he was the finest footballer he has ever seen. His favourite memory concerns a match against Leicester City. In the build-up to the match the Leicester full-back had been quoted in the papers as saying that they had a plan to stop Finney. Preston fans had heard of such plans before and they invariably involved defenders trying to kick their side's playmaker as high into the air as possible.

He takes up the story: "We played them in a night match and it was knee-deep in mud, which was to their advantage. In the first few minutes the ball went to Tom and the full-back came lunging in with a two-footed tackle. Tom just dropped his shoulder and neatly avoided him and all he connected with was the mud. Everybody cheered. It was like a bull fight with Tom the matador. People say players like Tom would find it difficult if they were playing today, but I think he would have relished getting more protection from the referee."

Wilf Wareing remembers Finney leading many defenders a merry dance, but can remember only one who seemed to be comfortable marking him and that was his fellow England international Tommy Banks, who played full-back for Bolton Wanderers and was a renowned tackler in the mould of Preston's own Tommy Docherty. The fan, though, may be mistaken. Certainly Banks himself thinks so. He admitted: "I always had trouble against Tom Finney. The man was a maestro. He had it all. I could only hope that they would play him on the other side or at centre-forward and then he would be someone else's problem."

Such was the pulling power of Finney, he remembers attendances would slump if the great man wasn't playing. "I remember a game in 1959 just before Finney finished and as I was walking towards the North End there were a lot of people walking back towards me. It wasn't a game where a full house was expected so I thought they couldn't have closed the gates and when I asked, a fellow said they'd heard Finney wasn't playing. They were not going to pay 1s 6d (8p) to watch Preston without Finney."

Joe Dunn said a factor in his decision to join Preston was the chance to play alongside Finney because he was a great player and a gent. "One thing I remember is that no matter how many times he got kicked he always got up and walked away. I never knew him retaliate and there was a lot of provocation. He did get kicked a lot. It was the only way defenders could stop him."

Marian Bell remembers that word leaking that Preston's greatest player would not be appearing was rare. "They weren't daft. They avoided making an announcement before the kick-off because it could reduce the crowd by 10,000. That was the draw of Finney. We were a one-man team, even though it is a team game. He did, though, have good service, as the other players knew what he wanted and needed. He wasn't just a superb player, but a wonderful man off the field as well. I've known him since the war. I used to go dancing with his wife before they were married. He is a gent is Tom."

Walter Horan adds his own tribute: "Tom Finney is the greatest footballer that I ever saw and he was rightly knighted for his services to soccer. He has had so many accolades and I remember just two from those who played against him. The legendary Manchester City goalkeeper Bert Trautmann said he was the 'finest forward I ever played against'. England's World Cup captain Bobby Moore said on his first sighting of Tom that he had never seen a forward who could control a game from outside-right."

The end for Finney came on April 30, 1960, in a 2-0 win against Luton Town on an emotion-charged occasion. Wilf Wareing was there and recalls: "It was very sad and very emotional. There were grown men crying. Everybody went to see him for the last time. It was not just Preston fans who turned up. People came from all over Lancashire. It was the passing of an era. In the years since, youngsters who were there will have told their children, and in time will tell their grandchildren, about the day that they saw the legend that was Tom Finney."

Finney himself remembers: "It was all very emotional and a sad day for me. My last game for Preston North End. I had played as a boy for them and now, at 38, I was finishing. It was a fair age to be playing League football in the First Division. The players all stood round in a circle and a band played *For He's A Jolly Good Fellow.* I was given a microphone and then had to say a few words. The game itself was something I didn't relish. It was so hard to concentrate and get tuned-in. The ceremony at the start hadn't helped. I had been playing centre-forward, but manager Cliff Britton had asked me where I wanted to play for my last game and, given the opportunity, I played my last game at outside-right.

With relegation in 1960-61 there were calls for a new manager and the name of Tom Finney was bandied about as the ideal candidate. The hope was that the man who had done so much to inspire North End as a player could now do the same from the manager's chair. Finney, though, was not to be seduced by such entreaties. He dismissed such an idea as either nonsense or wishful thinking and made clear he saw no future in football management, which he recognised was a precarious line of work and carried with it a high level of stress. Besides, as he pointed out, he had spent 15 years building up his plumbing business and was not going to turn his back on that venture.

Yet Finney's playing days were not quite over yet. There were the charity games, of course. Tommy Henderson, who organised the games for former Burnley players in which Finney often turned out, recalls: "At one stage he was playing so many charity games that his wife tried to put a halt to them. Tom had to keep a spare pair of boots at work so he could sneak off without her knowing. He was still really committed as well. I remember playing in a match in the Isle of Man with him and at half-time he was telling us where we were all going wrong."

Away from charity games there was to be one more appearance where he again took centre stage. The fixture was a European Cup-tie in 1963, against the Portuguese giants, Benfica, three years after he had hung up his boots as far as competitive football was concerned. Finney turned out for the Irish League club, Distillery.

He recalls: "I had kept myself trim with training the youngsters at North End and testimonial and charity matches, when George Eastham, the Distillery manager, said they were playing Benfica and would I turn out for them. At first I dismissed it out of hand by saying I wasn't fit, but George had seen reports of testimonial games. He wouldn't relent and I was finally persuaded, although I told him that, irrespective of the result, I would not be available for the return leg. It was a big match and although Benfica were at their peak and we were regarded as nonentities, it didn't turn out as everybody expected and we got a draw. That was a good result and everybody there was delighted. It was a novel way to end my career."

Then it was back to his plumbing business. He has retained his links with North End as president, which keeps him in touch with football and the club. He sees most of the home games and his appetite for the game has not been diminished over the years. In 1998 he received a knighthood that he says came out of the blue. "I was told a few weeks before I had been nominated and it was both a wonderful surprise and a great honour to me, the town of Preston and for football. Stan Matthews had got his, and Alf Ramsey, and now I was in their company." None could argue it is an honour fully deserved for a man who has given so much to football and been an ambassador for the game both as a player and in his subsequent retirement.

Expectations Frustrated

WITH the two previous seasons giving Preston fans plenty to cheer in first the League and then the Cup, their high expectations were to be frustrated in the two seasons between 1954 and 1956, when North End suffered a disappointing loss of form. If the first season was bad enough with a 14th-place finish, then the following year was even worse. It was all a far cry from the success they had been used to in the Fifties since winning promotion. Now the club found themselves too near the relegation dogfight for comfort.

In the 1954-55 season, memories of the Cup Final defeat were still painfully fresh and for players and fans alike there was the oft-repeated mantra of beaten Wembley teams that they would return the following year and make amends. Such hopes were to last no longer than the fourth round and a meeting with Sunderland that needed a replay to decide. Defeat against a high-flying side like Sunderland, who would finish fourth that season, and after a close-fought encounter was hard but bearable. The following season, though, North End bowed out at the first hurdle, losing 5-2 away to West Ham United, then in the bottom half of the Second Division.

However, there were some good wins for supporters to enjoy in 1954-55 season, but too often they were followed by defeats as the side failed to find the consistency needed to mount any sort of challenge for a high-table position. Yet it all started so well with 17 goals in three early-season wins. Cardiff City conceded five and seven goals in two matches, but in between there was an August 28 reverse away to Everton 1-0. There was still optimism, though, particularly after the opening match of the season when Manchester City were the visitors to Deepdale.

At the start of the new season, the crowds were still flocking to football matches in huge numbers, but a worrying trend of decline had already set in. The total League crowds for 1953-54 had been around a million less than for the previous season. Football was still the popular entertainment of the masses, but club chairmen were already sensing that the paying customers could not be taken for granted. The average attendance for the First Division, though, was still a healthy 34,967, a figure which today many clubs can only dream about. Transfer fees were already starting to climb and Preston, for one, resisted any temptation in the close season to over-extend the use of the cheque book. They bought only one player, Sammy Baird, from Clyde, who did not remain beyond his first season at North End. Baird joined Rangers and went on to win seven caps for Scotland.

Manchester City were popular visitors and not just because the club are near neighbours. In their last four encounters, the Lilywhites had notched up some big scores against their big-city rivals, winning 6-2, 2-0, 4-1 and 4-0. The fans arriving for the start of the new campaign were hoping for more of the same and were not to be disappointed. In a bid to reduce the workload on Finney, he had relinquished the captaincy and the side appeared keen to rely on him more sparingly, a policy perhaps dramatically brought home in the Cup Final when he had so failed to impress. The all-round general performance in which every forward took a greater share of responsibility had its reward with a 5-0 win that included a hat-trick for Charlie Wayman. The centre-forward, though, was to play only six games in the opening stages of the season before new manager Frank Hill transferred him to Middlesbrough. What made the decision seem particularly flawed was that the player had averaged a goal a game at the start of the campaign. Wayman went to Ayresome Park for £8,000 and his goals that season played a big part in keeping 'Boro in the Second Division.

Meanwhile, the Manchester City win had whetted appetites and raised hopes of another successful season, but such aspirations were to quickly evaporate. Home form was disappointing with 21 points being lost and one of the biggest reverses was a 4-2 defeat by Leicester City that was some revenge for Preston's triumph in their three-match Cup marathon the previous season. Finney again had a season troubled by injury and Cunningham missed seven League games with an injury received playing for Scotland against England in April. The longest unbeaten run was four games and by the end of the season, the fans were voting with their feet with only 13,328 watching the home game against Manchester United in the March, a game that was traditionally one of the major draws of the season.

Sunderland, dubbed 'the Bank of England side' at the time for their willingness to use the cheque book to try to buy success, were top of the table when they arrived on January 29 for their FA Cup fourth-round match with Preston, who had won at Second Division Fulham in the third round. After virtually building a new side the previous year, Sunderland had been tipped as the team to do well and they arrived high in confidence, strengthened by the knowledge that in each of their five previous Cup games with North End they had been the victors. The game was a hard-fought, entertaining encounter and the 3-3 result was a fair one. While generally played in the best of spirits, the match did bring Cunningham face to face again with former Burnley player Billy Elliott, with whom he had been involved in that bruising battle referred to earlier. Not surprisingly, there were a few full-blooded clashes between the two.

After Foster had squandered an opening engineered by Finney, the roles were reversed a few minutes later when it was Foster whose pass set up the scoring chance and Finney made no mistake. Four minutes later with North End enjoying the best of the play, Ted Purdon scored for the visitors to bring the sides level. Sunderland enjoyed a half-time lead, thanks to a goal by Ken Chisholm just before the break. After the restart, a shot by Morrison evaded everybody in a crowded penalty area to find the back of the net.

Minutes later, though, Len Shackleton restored Sunderland's lead, but the last word went to Foster and Preston had earned a draw. A trip to Roker Park, though, was always likely to be a daunting prospect.

Injuries forced Preston into desperate measures for the match with the decision to play full-back Joe Walton at centre-forward for the injured Dennis Hatsell. Originally it had been intended to play Mattinson, but he developed stomach problems that required hospital treatment. Finney was also out with a pulled muscle, so it was a sadly-depleted side that made the journey to the North East. In the first half, honours were even and no side put away their chances. However, it was a more determined Sunderland side that emerged after the break and it took only nine minutes for the 'Roker Roar' to be heard as a huge crowd of more than 57,000 had two goals to celebrate. Shackleton advanced down the right before crossing to the unmarked Chisholm, whose shot squeezed between post and upright for the opening score. Then Elliott beat Cunningham and crossed and it was Chisholm in the right place at the right time to profit with a header. It was the North East side who would advance to meet Swansea in the next round.

The League campaign drew to an unspectacular close with Preston losing their last home game, against Aston Villa 3-0. Yet if 14th place was a disappointment for the fans, the final game of the season, away to Charlton Athletic, gave supporters a glimmer of what North End were capable of, if only they had been more consistent. The official verdict touted at the time was that it had been an exasperating season as the only thing consistent about Preston was the team's unpredictability. The Lilywhites travelled to The Valley and before a crowd of only 15,120 they triumphed 4-0 with a superb display that belied their place in the table. The team played with skill and confidence and the score could have been higher but for some fine work by Sam Bartram in the Charlton goal. As it was, Ken Waterhouse, later to make a decent living in the lower divisions, scored a hat-trick and there was one for Baxter in a brilliant exhibition. It set the players up nicely for a tour of Scotland before the hard work in the Football League resumed in August.

After several seasons when he formed a much feared half-back line with Tommy Docherty and Willie Forbes, the Australian centre-half Joe Marston decided to return to his native country in 1955 after notching up nearly 200 first-team appearances. It provided the opening for another player who was to become a popular figure with the Deepdale faithful. The departure of Marston gave Joe Dunn his chance of regular first-team football in the 1955-56 season.

Dunn had been signed from Scottish club Clyde in July 1951, for £1,500, but veteran Willie Forbes ensured his first-team outings were comparatively rare. He had been keen to join the club, having been stationed at nearby Kirkham while serving in the RAF during the war and he liked the town and praised the friendliness of the people. The club had just been relegated but he recalls there was a feeling they wouldn't be in the Second Division for long, and so it proved.

However, it was to be his misfortune to arrive as a regular in the first team when the side were struggling and the 1955-56 season saw Preston too close to the League basement for comfort. That they pulled clear was in no small part due to the defensive qualities of the defender. With First Division clubs enjoying large playing squads, such a long apprenticeship as Dunn served was by no means unusual and meant the player was completely at ease with the club's style and knew his team-mates' strengths and weaknesses when he did finally graduate to regular first-team football.

The centre-half had, not surprisingly, the requisite heading and tackling skills for the position and was a regular until the 1960-61 season. An injury to Tony Singleton gave him another chance after a spell in the Reserves, but a 5-1 defeat at Sheffield Wednesday in February 1961 marked his final match. In all he made 239 League and Cup appearances for the club. When he finished playing for Preston he went to Morecambe as player-manager. He still lives in the town.

He remembers it was a good time to be playing football and the crowd were appreciative and knowledgeable. There was not the pressure on players there is today when a couple of defeats can lead to a call for heads to roll. Rather the supporters liked a good game of football and although they were disappointed to lose, if they felt that they had been given value for their money, then most of them accepted the result. In his first season as a regular, that attitude was rather fortunate.

"I can remember matches where we were applauded off, even though we had lost," he said. "We were struggling a bit in the first season I was a regular, but I don't think we had suddenly become a bad team overnight. The results didn't go our way, but we felt they would come right. I enjoyed every game I played. Being a footballer is a wonderful way to earn a living and I met a lot of nice people and was made very welcome in the town. Preston is a friendly club. We met the supporters after the games and often they would want your autograph. There was also a good atmosphere in the dressing-room."

The season was an aberration in Preston's record during the Fifties. They finished fourth from bottom and, but for good runs at crucial times, could have been in far more serious trouble. Yet it had all started so well. The opening match of the season had seen North End earn an impressive 4-0 win over Everton at Goodison with new recruit Tommy Thompson getting a goal. Preston then suffered only one defeat in their first six matches and supporters anticipated another season of top-half-of-the-table football with perhaps the chance to challenge for glory. It was not to be and their form slumped.

Thompson had begun his career with Newcastle United before being sold to Aston Villa where he quickly established a goalscoring reputation. Preston secured his services for £27,000 and he was to form a devastating partnership with Tom Finney from 1955 to 1960. He announced his arrival in the best possible way with that goal within two minutes away to Everton. There were greater glories to come. During his five seasons, Thompson and Finney between them scored 203 League goals, which was no mean feat at the highest level. He twice played for England, having been selected once while with Villa and then again while at Preston, in 1957 against Scotland at Wembley.

He had started his career at Newcastle United after learning his skills in junior soccer. He turned in some good performances in the lower sides and often before fair-sized attendances. He remembers the reserve team could get gates of 15,000. After breaking into the first team and playing more than 20 games, he saw his future at St

James's Park. He hadn't wanted to leave the North East, but had no choice in the matter, as was the way in this era. To refuse to move would have meant being cast into the football wilderness as Newcastle wouldn't have given him any first-team opportunities or let him play anywhere else.

He said: "I was disappointed. You never want to leave your home-town team and I hoped to make it at Newcastle. If they had waited a few more months, as I got stronger and more used to first-team football, they might have changed their minds. I did, though, go straight into the Villa first team and I was never out of it for five years. I enjoyed my time there and having played at Villa Park and St James's Park, I was performing before some of the best supporters in the country. When I said I was ready for a change and a new challenge, Villa let me go for £27,000 so they made a good profit out of me. I got a £20 signing-on fee and that was it."

Thompson added: "I knew that at the time Preston had a lot of good players and were a good footballing side. The crowds were smaller. But the maximum wage meant the money was the same. I never knew of the pay barrier being broken but it was rumoured that players from Scotland got a financial incentive. Whatever the fee was, they put an extra £1,000 on it for the player. It was all unofficial, but it happened."

The manager who signed Thompson was Frank Hill. "He was all right and was there for a couple of years after I joined. Managers like Frank didn't come on to the training ground like they do today. He wasn't a tracksuit manager but was more concerned with the business side of the club and dealt with the chairman and the directors. I didn't have a lot of dealings with him, but he had been a good player in his day."

Indeed, Hill was a Scotland international who played in the great Arsenal team of the Thirties, with whom he won three League championship medals before playing for both Blackpool and Southampton. He was a coach and assistant trainer at North End before the outbreak of war. After the hostilities ended, he was player-manager at Crewe Alexandra and then manager at Burnley before returning to Deepdale as manager in 1954. He stayed for three years before taking up a coaching appointment in Baghdad. On his return, he managed Notts County and then Charlton Athletic before retiring in 1965.

The move to Preston also gave Thompson the chance to team up with Tom Finney. He had played alongside him before. The two were in a Football League side that beat the League of Ireland 4-1 with Finney at outside-right and himself at inside-right. Thompson, then with Villa, scored all four goals for his side and it proved his passport into the England side. When he came to Deepdale, he was confident that the two could rekindle the understanding they developed in that game, and so it proved.

Although generally results during Thompson's first season at Preston were disappointing, there were still some days for the fans to savour. On October 29, Preston travelled to Blackpool and took the usual sizeable travelling support. They were to give those fans plenty to cheer. With Finney, Walton and Forbes all back in action, Preston had their strongest side available and a 6-2 victory was the result. All the forwards got in on the scoring act with Hatsell getting two as Blackpool suffered their first home defeat of the season. A contributory factor in the scoreline was undoubtedly the loss of the Seasiders' goalkeeper George Farm in the opening minutes. For the home fans there was the remarkable conversation topic of having their goalkeeper score one of the goals. With no substitutes and teams reluctant to be reduced to ten men, Farm was sent upfield as a centre-forward. His header from a Matthews cross produced the goal and a mighty cheer from the Bloomfield Road crowd. By the time Farm was forced to hand over the 'keeper's jersey, Preston were already two goals ahead as a paralysed nerve in his arm had rendered the 'keeper a liability, prompting the decision to find a volunteer to go between the posts. The job fell to full-back Jimmy Armfield, who conceded another four. Although Farm's loss was a key factor, Preston did enough to give their supporters the belief they would have won anyway, although perhaps the score might have been kept more respectable from Blackpool's viewpoint.

Another team that the crowd loved to see North End do well against was Manchester United. They were to finish the season as champions, but when they visited in January it was the home side who gained the plaudits and the points in a game that also marked Finney's 300th League game. Former United man Eddie Lewis scored the first goal after eight minutes when he seized on a mistake by 'keeper Ray Wood, who failed to collect a Tommy Thompson shot cleanly. Despite the muddy conditions there was some skilful football on show and United pulled level through Bill Whelan with a shot from an acute angle. Two minutes after the interval, Preston were back in front thanks to Thompson. When the same player was fouled by Duncan Edwards five minutes from time, Foster scored with the free-kick.

While for this one year results may have been disappointing, Marian Bell remembers the whole Fifties period as a wonderful time to be watching soccer. If the football was good, fans could put up with the results not always going their way. Winning was not the all-important issue it has now become. Relations with other fans were good and everybody appreciated good play and skilful players, whether it was the opposition or your own team.

She remembers: "There was good banter and none of the filth you get now. We gave the team encouragement and there were fans as staunch in their support as anybody today but without being unpleasant to anyone. There were big crowds as well. Against teams like Manchester United and Arsenal, when there was a huge crowd the kids would be handed over the top of heads to get them to the front where they could get a view of the game and be safe."

The 1955-56 season ended with Preston in 19th place, only one point clear of relegation. Huddersfield Town and Sheffield United went down, Aston Villa being saved by virtue of the fact that their goal-average was 0.2 per cent better than Huddersfield's. And to think that in their penultimate match of the season, Villa had won 1-0 at Deepdale.

Manager Frank Hill could hardly have expected to survive such a poor season, and the departure of Charlie Wayman still haunted him. Indeed, Hill had issued a statement saying that as Wayman was nearing 34 and the club wanted to be fair to him, they thought he would appreciate the opportunity to return to his North East roots.

The fans certainly did not appreciate it and four games into the 1956-57 season, all of which had ended in defeat, Cliff Britton took over at Deepdale. Britton, a great name for Everton before the war, had then managed Burnley before taking over at Goodison Park. In 1956 he resigned, complaining of undue interference from the Everton board. In August that year he became manager of Preston North End.

Back To Their Best

THE two seasons between 1956 and 1958 saw Proud Preston regain the form of earlier in the decade and reach heights in the top flight which, to date, they have not seen again. Despite that dreadful start to 1956-57, they finished third in the table and were embroiled in a mammoth Cup run that saw six games played in the three rounds they competed in. The following season North End went one better in the League, finishing runners-up behind a Wolves side who won the title by five points. For the last time Preston were a force to be reckoned with in the football world.

The arrival of Frank O'Farrell from West Ham United in November 1956, coincided with a 15-game unbeaten run starting with a 3-1 win over Manchester City on December 1 and ending with the FA Cup replay defeat against Arsenal. Taking the Cup-ties out of the equation, it was 16 League games before Preston tasted defeat. It was a superb display and a far cry from the opening games of the season when Preston went four matches without gaining a point. They had opened the season with Spurs visiting Deepdale and the Londoners inflicted a 4-1 defeat. Tottenham would finish above Preston on goal-average when the season closed. Chelsea beat Preston 1-0 at Stamford Bridge and Manchester United did a midweek double over their Lancashire neighbours, winning 3-1 at Deepdale and 3-2 at Old Trafford, thanks to a Dennis Violett hat-trick. That was on August 29; the following day, Britton was appointed.

O'Farrell was the first signing of manager Cliff Britton since his arrival at the club and he proved a more than adequate replacement for Willie Forbes at left-half. No money changed hands in the deal with West Ham taking centre-forward Eddie Lewis in a straight exchange deal. It was an auspicious start for the man who had already notched up 210 League and Cup games for the Hammers as he scored in his opening game for North End, against Manchester City at Deepdale. He departed in 1961 as one of a dozen players whose services were dispensed with at the end of the relegation season. He had made 129 League and Cup appearances. He was to become well-known as a manager, particularly when he took probably the highest-profile club manager's job in the game, at Manchester United.

Preston's change of fortunes had been signalled when Cardiff City were the visitors on September 1. Six goals without reply ended the points drought in emphatic fashion and sparked the revival that saw the side in the title chase, albeit a good way behind a rampant Manchester United, who would win the championship by an eight-point margin. The Welsh side found their opponents had suddenly discovered a confidence and teamwork conspicuously absent up until their arrival. All six goals were scored by the 46th minute, as the visitors were taken apart. Supporters who had doubted them earlier in the season were now won over to the cause, while those who had stood by the side were vindicated for their loyalty. Indeed, the score could have been greater. If only the upsurge in form had arrived earlier, before the Old Trafford side were able to take all four League points off North End in their August encounters.

Thereafter, the faithful saw some glorious displays with some results to cherish, although there was also a 4-0 defeat at Bloomfield Road as North End came off worse in the fluctuating fortunes that made the old feud with their great rivals so compelling. There were still plenty of plus points, though. Struggling Sunderland travelled to Deepdale and were on the end of a six-goal hiding without even the consolation of a goal for their travelling fans.

The Wearsiders had been something of a bogey team for Preston down the years. North End did have a 6-2 win in October 1953, but in general the Lancashire side often came off worse in the contests. League meetings between the two began in 1891 but it was the visit of Sunderland on November 3, 1956 which was to see North End inflict a record defeat. Having outclassed the visitors from the start, there were even complaints in some quarters that Preston slackened their efforts once they were five up! The handful of goals had come in the first half and there was just the one in the second period against a defence that had been run ragged. After the break, Finney failed to connect with a header, Sammy Taylor missed an open goal and a Baxter shot went just wide to spare Sunderland further blushes. There was a chasm of difference in class between the two sides. The experiment of playing Finney at centre-forward was clearly working. He scored two goals, one from a penalty, which brought his tally to 11 goals in 11 games. Others getting in on the act included Tommy Thompson, who collected a hat-trick, and Taylor.

Sammy Taylor was another of the Scottish contingent to be lured south to the Lancashire town and he signed from Falkirk in May 1955, for £8,500. He made his debut at the start of the new season, when his primary role was to stand-in for either Finney or Angus Morrison, and he was to eventually replace the latter. With Finney being played at centre-forward, Taylor switched from left to right wing and was a great success. In the two seasons when Preston hit their peak, he scored 26 goals. He remained at Deepdale until April 1961, when he joined Carlisle United. His career ended at Stockport County where the manager was one Willie Cunningham.

The Sunderland game was not the only thrashing handed out by an, at times, rampant North End. Portsmouth's troubles near the foot of the table were not helped by a 7-1 pasting at Deepdale in which Taylor scored a hat-trick. Charlton Athletic were to finish bottom of the table, but they enjoyed two thrilling games with Preston that both saw seven goals scored, with North End winning by the odd goal on both occasions. A measure of the side's goalscoring ability is reflected in the fact that Finney and Thompson scored 57 League and Cup goals between them.

Sometimes, though, the sublime play of Preston did not produce an avalanche of goals. They did, however, usually still manage to provide entertainment. Such was the case when Birmingham City were the visitors in the midst of an FA Cup-tie against Sheffield Wednesday that needed three games to decide. The home side scored only once, but it could have been many more and the near misses brought groans and gasps from the crowd. The luckiest escape for Birmingham came when a powerful header by Baxter struck a post and rolled along the goal-line before it was hacked clear. Tommy Thompson got the goal that secured the points.

Finney was proving his versatility at centre-forward and was clearly still at the height of his powers. That was confirmed when he was voted Footballer of the Year for the second time. He was the first player to be given the award twice. Unfortunately, there were to be no major club honours on the playing field for the great man.

It was in the FA Cup that the club caught the imagination of the Preston public with some epic games, although there was to be ultimate disappointment. For the third round, North End faced First Division opposition in Sheffield Wednesday. At least the Lilywhites had the advantage of a home draw. Playing at Deepdale in the Cup was something of a luxury for North End. In the ten seasons since the resumption of League football, the Wednesday game was only their tenth at home, and two of those were replays. The tie also brought together the sides who had contested the 1954 semi-final at Maine Road, which Preston won 2-0.

In heavy conditions neither side could find the net in a game that still managed to be entertaining. In the centre of the Wednesday defence Don McEvoy was able to keep Finney in check, while at the other end the rare Wednesday forays were snuffed out by the home defenders. With the rain and mud counting against Preston's attempts to play good passing football, it meant a replay at Hillsborough. More than 60,000 were crammed into the ground for the replay. They twice saw North End fight back to get on level terms in a 2-2 draw that ensured the game would go to a second replay at Goodison Park. Such had been the interest in the game that the *Lancashire Evening Post* offices were inundated with callers keen to know the progress of the match. At one point the switchboard was so jammed it was feared that the journalist filing the match report would be unable to get through.

A 5-1 scoreline at Goodison was flattering to North End but the result ensured a fourth-round tie against Second Division Bristol Rovers. It was Wednesday who took the lead but as the game progressed the superior play of the Preston side began to swing the tie in their favour. Taylor levelled the scores after 13 minutes with a shot from short range after the ball was not cleared by the defenders. By half-time it was 3-1 with O'Farrell and Baxter both scoring. Any doubts about the result were quickly banished by the right foot of Thompson, whose shot made it four. The same player was on target with a header to give a comfortable gloss to the score. Those in charge of the coffers were also happy. The three games had grossed around £18,000 gate money.

Bristol Rovers were not a side to be taken lightly on their Eastville ground. None knew that more than the Preston players who had been on the receiving end of a Cup shock five years earlier, when they lost 2-0 with a side missing Finney through injury. This time the legend did take to the field and his two goals in a 4-1 win ensured North End's Cup dreams did not, for the second time, end in the infamous heavy mud that had bogged down many Cup hopes, not least those of Manchester United who had the previous season lost 4-0 at Eastville.

The football fates were kind enough to hand Preston another home draw for the fifth round. They were not so generous in their choice of opponents, however, with Arsenal the visitors. Preston had done the double over the Gunners in the League, but they were to finish fifth in the table and would be no easy opponents in the Cup.

Shortly after dawn on the day of the match, the first of the Arsenal supporters arrived to find Preston covered by a blanket of snow. At that time the London club boasted the largest supporters' club in the country and they were keen to make themselves heard with bells, rattles and their red and white colours. They left onlookers in no doubt where their favours lay. Local cafes did a roaring trade as they waited to make their way to Deepdale. In all, more than 3,000 made the journey from the capital.

The visiting fans had plenty to cheer in the first half as their side went 2-0 up and Preston looked down and out of the Cup. It was the worst possible start for North End when, to the dismay of the majority of the 39,608 crowd, in the first minute Dunn slipped as he tried to clear a centre and put the ball through his own net. The same player nearly put colleague Cunningham out of the game when an attempted kick of the ball missed and hit the player instead. Fortunately Cunningham was able to resume after treatment and he played a magnificent game. Finney scored for Preston, but the half belonged to the Gunners with the score 3-1 in their favour at the break. It was left to the magic of Finney to bring North End back into the match. He scored with a header and could easily have had two more, hitting the bar and seeing a shot cleared off the line. A shot by Thompson ensured a replay and that Preston's Cup marathon would continue.

Thompson missed the replay, having pulled a thigh muscle, and Waterhouse made one of his rare appearances for the Preston first team. However, there was better news when it came to Baxter and Cunningham, both of whom passed fitness tests. The match had caught the imagination in London with more than 61,000 packed into Highbury, a crowd boosted by the decision of both clubs not to allow the game to be televised. The days when television moguls could dictate where they went and when games kicked-off were still a long way off. The view among most clubs was that the TV cameras could only hit attendances.

None expressed that opinion more forcibly than Bob Lord, controversial chairman of Preston's Lancashire rivals Burnley and senior vice-president of the Football Association. Lord was adamant that television was bad for football and that attendances would suffer. He felt television did not give enough for what it got. One wonders what his view would be now, with the astronomical figures being paid by television for the rights to screen more and more games. He particularly feared that live television would arrive, coupled with leading players as commentators and that would be a big lure to keep the average fan in the armchair in front of the box, rather than going through the turnstiles. He might have had his faults, but he could be a pretty shrewd judge. The figure again is that 40 million watched football live in the post-war years. Only half that number pay to see the game today.

In Preston's replay against Arsenal, the best chances of the early exchanges fell to the visitors. Finney cut in from the right wing and shot, only for the ball to hit the bar and rebound out to where a grateful defender hacked it clear. Generally, though, the first half had been disappointing and lacked the passion of a Cup-tie. Nerves and a sense of the importance of the occasion perhaps took their toll. It was just after the hour when Arsenal opened the scoring with the unmarked Bill Dodgin rising high to head home a corner. For the seventh time in the season, Preston were a goal behind in a Cup-tie. Six minutes later, Arsenal increased their lead and made North End's task even harder when a telling break and cross by Derek Tapscott was met by David Herd who scored a spectacular goal that left Fred Else in the Preston goal with no chance. Les Dagger came off his wing to fire a powerful shot past Jack Kelsey to narrow the deficit, but it was as near as North End were to get, despite some good chances.

The following year was to see Preston go one better in the League and finish runners-up for the second time in the decade. However, in the Cup there was to be disappointment.

This was to be the year that Bolton Wanderers returned to Wembley and made amends for the defeat they had suffered five years earlier at the hands of Blackpool in the match dubbed 'The Matthews Final'. The first step on their journey was a visit to Preston and for both sides the fixture was as tough as they come. Unfortunately for North End, the visit to Deepdale was to bring out the best in their opponents who produced one of the finest displays of their season to gain a comfortable 3-0 victory.

Around 40,000 were squeezed into Deepdale and the home fans were confident of seeing their side to victory. The League encounter had seen North End comfortable winners, 3-0 against a side that would finish in the bottom half of the table. When the side visited Burnden Park for the penultimate game of the season, the result would be even more emphatic with a 4-0 win. This, though, was the

Cup and League form can be thrown out of the window. Preston's Cup dreams were about to be shattered. After a goalless first half, three goals in 15 minutes of the second period saw Bolton through. It was a fully deserved win with two goals for Ray Parry and one for Dennis Stevens.

Bolton and England goalkeeper Eddie Hopkinson recalls his feelings before the Preston game: "When we saw the draw there was a feeling that it couldn't have been any harder for the third round of the Cup. To go there when Tom Finney was at his prime and win 3-0 was a remarkable result. That performance set us on our way and gave us the confidence to believe we could go all the way to Wembley."

The Wanderers and England full-back Tommy Banks also approached the tie with some trepidation. In a modern world of physically big players, he has no doubt that there would still have been a place for Finney. Words fail him when he comes to describe the talent of the North End star. And he admits that he rarely had a good game against him. "I never played Tom Finney well and it was a god-send to me that day that they played him on the left and Roy Hartle stopped him. By the time they switched wings in the second half, Roy had taken the edge off him. That was a good win and it had been a hard start for us."

Finney himself recalls: "We were playing well and should have done better but in the Cup it is all on the day. Nat Lofthouse was a tower of strength. We were fated to often lose to the side that went on to win the Cup. It happened with both Aston Villa and Charlton as well. I suppose we were a lucky omen, but there wasn't much luck in it for us."

Tommy Thompson reflects on a career in which he was destined to be unlucky in the Cup. He left Newcastle in 1950 and missed out on their three visits to Wembley. He departed from Aston Villa in 1955 and they lifted the trophy in 1957. When he finished at Preston in 1961, they were to go to the Twin Towers in 1964. He had, of course, joined in 1955 and that was the year after their FA Cup Final meeting with West Bromwich Albion. The meeting with Bolton was to be another unfortunate chapter in his FA Cup experiences.

He said: "We were red-hot favourites and had already had a comfortable win in the League. At the last minute, Cliff Britton changed the team. Earlier in the season, Tom wasn't fit so he played Dennis Hatsell at centre-forward. The previous week we had beaten Portsmouth without Tom, but now he was back he should have played him at centre-forward. He now switched him to outside-left. It was one game where the atmosphere in the dressing-room before the game was all wrong. We just weren't right when we went out. The following week we played West Brom and Tom was back at centre-forward. We won that game and went from strength to strength. Yet for the penultimate game of the season, against Bolton, Britton switched again and brought Hatsell back to centre-forward. It was just to prove a point. He wasn't even at the match himself because he was on a scouting mission."

The League season was a high-water mark for Preston, one that they have never come close to emulating since. The team were at their peak and proved more than a match for any side in the land. With Tommy Thompson scoring 34 League goals and his strike partner Tom Finney a further 26, some big scores were again inflicted on opponents. Wolves were an impressive side and would win the League not just this season, but also the next. They succeeded in doing the double over their nearest challengers, which severely dented Preston's hopes of catching them, but throughout the season North End gamely tried to challenge, although by the end they were five points adrift.

In a season of big wins, none stands out more than the result against Birmingham City. The 8-0 victory was Preston's biggest of the century in a First Division match and those who saw it are quick to make clear it was not a flattering result. On a day when everything went right, the Preston team achieved sublime heights of football. They were a clear eight goals better than their hapless opponents. At the end, the defeated players congratulated the Preston players in a warm show of sportsmanship. Birmingham were not a poor side and would finish the season comfortably in mid-table. In goal they had Gil Merrick, who had won 23 full England caps, although it also has to be said that in their very next game, City conceded five goals at Molineux.

The Preston performance included two hat-tricks, one for Taylor and another for Thompson, as well as a pair for Finney. Perhaps this was one of Finney's best-ever chances to get the hat-trick that always eluded him in his League and Cup career with North End, but it was not to be.

A hat-trick for Thompson came as no surprise. He scored in 11 consecutive League games to establish a new club record and also scored the last goal in a 3-0 defeat of Arsenal in the last game of the season that brought up the magic 100-goal tally for Preston in 1957-58. It might not have added up to any trophies, but it certainly produced a lot of excitement for the supporters.

Looking back on the season that so nearly earned a place for the Lilywhites' in sporting history, Thompson says: "You can always point to one or two games where points were lost that would have made all the difference. However, I thought then, and still do, that although we had a good squad we were short of one or two players in key areas where we should have bought to strengthen. I think with a couple more players we could have lifted the title. For example, the responsibility for goalscoring tended to fall on myself and Tom Finney. If we had got somebody else who could have weighed-in with ten to 15 goals a season, that would have given us a good crack at League and Cup. We did, though, have a good run for two or three years and were always competing."

Finney recalls: "We had some outstanding individuals in the side and yet a great team spirit as well. Everybody worked for each other and as a team we were at a peak. At times we produced some wonderful football. Against Birmingham everything just gelled and we were brilliant. Everybody was at the top of their game. Afterwards I looked back on that match, and on some of the other times during that season when it came right, with great satisfaction that we had turned in such a performance. I was not just pleased personally but that as a team we had achieved that level of football. When we played like that, I think we could have beaten anyone."

Roland Jessop still recalls the disappointment of the 1957-58 season when Preston missed out on the title. Winning the League championship would have been just reward for a great team who had got where they were by playing an exciting style of football. He believes that few people, other than Wolves fans, would have begrudged the Lancashire side the title if it had come to pass. Sadly it was not to be.

He said: "It wasn't just Tom Finney but the whole side that peaked. I remember seeing a picture when they first signed Willie Cunningham and he was there, bow-legged and looking nothing like a footballer, but what a player he turned out to be and he had a great season that year. He never missed a game. There were others as well. As the season progressed, the whole town thought they might do it, and to lose out was cruel. Tom, for one, deserved some reward for the performances he turned in and the pleasure he brought to football fans everywhere."

A Sad And Rapid Decline

AFTER two years of challenging for the League championship, the decline of Preston North End was to be swift and inexorable. While other clubs, even today, may linger in the top flight as permanent relegation candidates facing seasons of struggle, the demise of the once-great North End was all too rapid. After being among the top handful of clubs in the country, within three seasons they were relegated and would never return, at least up to the time of writing. For fans brought up on life at the top, it was a hard pill to swallow.

After hitting their peak as League runners-up, Preston started the 1958-59 campaign with optimism that was to prove unfounded with a 12th-place finish. For now, though, the ignominy of what was to shortly follow was still far from the fans' minds. The season had its landmarks. For Tommy Thompson there was the milestone of his 100th League goal for Preston, scored against his former club Aston Villa. The season also saw the departure of Tommy Docherty for Arsenal after his sterling service in a Preston shirt. The move was not completed until after the opening match of the season, when Preston entertained the Gunners and enjoyed a 2-1 win.

Tommy Thompson recalls: "Time was starting to take its toll. Players were all getting old together and there were no suitable replacements being bought or coming through the ranks. Tommy

Docherty left and was never adequately replaced and that was true with others as well. Cliff Britton tried to fill in with players rather than getting the cheque book out and getting some quality. The successful clubs have players coming through to replace those who are getting to the end of their careers. It guarantees succession and keeps them at the top. It's like a conveyor belt. Preston didn't have that. They had a good team that declined. I think in North End's case the success had largely happened by good luck rather than good management. It wasn't just the clubs with money who stayed at the peak of the game. Burnley, for one, always seemed able to turn out good players."

However, he said that unlike Burnley, with their renowned Gawthorpe training ground and their superb scouting and coaching regime, Preston had poor training facilities that even in the Fifties were out of date. In the final analysis he thinks it was Britton who oversaw the decline of the team without doing enough to turn it round, even though the club obviously had the money with attendances still good.

Indeed, in a largely disappointing season the results against Arsenal were to be one of the highlights. Preston completed the double over the Londoners with an identical 2-1 scoreline at Highbury. Preston had been forced to throw two youngsters into the fray due to injuries. Both regular goalkeeper Fred Else and reserve Alan Kelly were sidelined, so between the posts was a 16-year-old amateur, John Barton. After 134 consecutive League games, Joe Walton was injured and John O'Neill got his chance.

Barton may have been the most nervous player on the field, but it was his opposite number, Welsh international Jack Kelsey, who was first to pick the ball out of the net with Preston scoring after 14 minutes. Thompson got the better of his former team-mate Docherty and gave centre-forward Hatsell the chance of a shot from an acute angle which he duly netted. The same player had his second on the half-hour when he got his head to a Derek Mayers cross. North End may have been understrength, but they were two up against a side that would finish third in the League. In the 39th minute, Scotland winger Jackie Henderson gave young Barton no chance with a shot.

Yet it was the young goalkeeper who earned the plaudits in the second half with a string of saves that ensured the points were Preston's. His parents were in the stand, proudly watching a remarkable debut.

During the season, the North End defence was not always so secure. In each of nine games, Preston conceded four goals or more. Perhaps a more telling statistic on Preston's fortunes during the season was that because of injury, Tom Finney managed only 16 League games. It was to be his last international season. Against Northern Ireland in Belfast on October 4, 1958 he scored his 30th goal, an England record. Two weeks later, at Wembley, he bowed out in the 5-0 victory over the USSR, in a game in which Nat Lofthouse equalled Finney's England scoring record. Said Finney, "It was sad playing my last international but I was so grateful for the memories, for having played with and against so many great players, and for making so many friends."

To add to the disappointment of the fans, Christmas saw a double defeat against their old adversaries Blackpool. On Christmas Day they travelled to Bloomfield Road and lost 4-2 with Bill Perry collecting a hat-trick to the delight of the home crowd. Any hopes of revenge the following day quickly disappeared with boyhood Preston fan Ray Charnley putting childhood loyalties to one side to bag a brace for the visitors and Hugh Kelly getting a third.

Three draws in the last four games of the season were the kind of results that summed up the average nature of the campaign. Preston's flirtation with the top of the table had been brief. The championship was won by Wolves with Manchester United runners-up. They were two teams who, throughout this era, consistently turned in good results thanks to the money their large following generated. To win a League title generally requires strength in depth that small-town teams like Preston could rarely afford.

The best chance of silverware was in the Cup. Derby County were despatched 4-2 at Deepdale after Preston had travelled to the Baseball Ground and gained a 2-2 draw. Derby, then a mediocre Second Division side, had threatened to pull off a shock on a snow-covered pitch. Jack Parry, brother of Bolton's Ray, put the Rams ahead after only two minutes. Preston drew level three minutes later and then George Darwin had restored Derby's lead after 19 minutes, by which time Preston had missed a penalty. With 12 minutes remaining, Preston were looking a Cup shock in the face when Derby's Albert Mays tried a long back-pass, the ball slowed down on the snow and was turned into a superb defence-splitting through ball on to which ran Dennis Hatsell to save the day. After the replay was first postponed because of fog, Preston eased through in comfort at Deepdale.

A narrow win over Third Division Bradford City set up a marathon Cup-tie against Bolton Wanderers that was to go to three games and be watched by nearly 150,000 people.

Tommy Thompson remembers: "We had some great tussles with Wanderers in the League and this was a Cup-tie that could have gone either way. We travelled to Burnden Park for the first tie and it was the only time I captained the side apart from on a pre-season tour to South Africa once. What sticks out in my mind was that we were awarded a penalty. Both our regular penalty-takers, Tom Finney and Dennis Hatsell, weren't playing.

"I turned round and all the rest of the team were on the halfway line. They didn't want to know. I had to take the penalty and scored it. We drew that game 2-2 and then it was a draw again at Deepdale, 1-1. They got the only goal when we played at Ewood Park. You need a bit of luck in the Cup and it went their way."

The following year, the 1959-60 campaign marked the last for the great Tom Finney, whose supreme talent had been such a factor in securing Preston's place at the very top of the English game. The match against Luton Town on April 30, 1960, was his last for the club in a season where he was leading goalscorer with 17 League and four Cup goals to his credit. A 2-0 victory was seemingly incidental as the football world paid tribute to one of the greats. It would have been wonderful if his curtain-call had been at Wembley in a Cup Final rather than a League game against Luton Town, but a sixth-round defeat at the hands of Aston Villa, 2-0, put paid to those hopes. Unlike Stanley Matthews, there was to be no Cup winners' medal for Tom Finney.

The season had started badly with the first three games drawn and only one win in the first six games, a 2-1 success at Newcastle United. Two wins, when North End scored four goals against Manchester United and Blackburn Rovers in successive weeks at the end of September and the beginning of October, were sandwiched between two heavy defeats when they conceded five against both Tottenham Hotspur and Manchester City with just one goal as scant consolation in both games. The old problem of inconsistency was back to haunt them, with the team capable of swinging from the sublime to the mediocre in successive weeks. Preston were to make an improvement on the previous season with a ninth-place finish, but hopes of challenging the eventual champions, neighbouring Burnley, for the title were never a realistic ambition.

In one game they combined their problem of leaking too many goals with their capacity to score a few as well. When Chelsea were the visitors, it meant no League points, but no shortage of entertainment. The final score was 5-4 to the visitors and Roland Jessop, for one, has no doubts as to the quality of the football on show when he says: "It was one of the best games I ever saw at Deepdale. It was a cracking game that ebbed and flowed. We were used to watching the best players every week and this time it was Jimmy Greaves who put on a show."

When the teams had met in the first game of the season, the score was 4-4 – Greaves scored a hat-trick – and it was to be another thriller when battle was resumed at Deepdale on December 19, before a disappointing crowd of only 15,775. Chelsea had lost their last four games and with Preston riding high in the League, the Londoners were not the favourites. That, though, did not take into account the talents of Greaves. He opened the scoring after 14 minutes when he caught the defence napping with a well-timed break. A minute later, Tommy Thompson brought North End level when he beat the 'keeper to a cross and shot home. A pass by Thompson enabled Dave Sneddon to give Preston the lead with a shot from an acute angle. Two goals for Greaves in a three-minute spell returned the lead to Chelsea before the break. The fans might have hoped for a Preston fightback, but Greaves was having none of it. There were two more

Chelsea goals. And two more for the supremely-talented Greaves to give him five on the day. To the delight of the crowd, North End rose to the challenge of a three-goal deficit and Thompson collected two more to bring up his hat-trick, but the equaliser was to prove elusive. It was, though, great entertainment.

The end of Preston North End as a top-flight side came in the 1960-61 season, just a year after Tom Finney's retirement. It was, though, not just the loss of the great man himself that spelled the end. The veterans of the side that had peaked three years before were starting to see age take its toll and there was not the quality in place to step into their boots. Perhaps Finney, if he had still been around, may have been able to conjure enough of the old magic to keep Preston off the foot of the table. It was not to be and, in any case, would surely have merely postponed the inevitable.

Joe Dunn recalls the moment that relegation was confirmed as the lowest point in his career. There were some players in tears in the dressing-room and others just sat in stunned silence. Dunn himself waited ten minutes before making his way to the bath. For any club to be relegated is a blow, but what made it worse was that it had happened to a side like Preston, who only a few seasons before had been challenging at the other end of the table. Nobody, including the player himself, could guess that it was to be the end of Preston's tenure in the top flight up to the present day.

Dunn's own contribution in the relegation season was limited to four appearances as he was kept on the sidelines by Tony Singleton, who he describes as a 'big strong lad'. An injury to Singleton saw the veteran recalled for a game at Sheffield Wednesday on February 4. Preston lost 5-1 and the player admits: "I didn't play well. Something went wrong and I don't know what. I suppose I guessed after that it was probably my last game. I'd only been brought back because of an injury. It certainly wasn't a good way to end my Preston career."

It is useful to look at the basement of the First Division in 1960-61. Preston were bottom, but occupying two of the four places above them were fellow small-town Lancashire clubs. Just escaping the drop by a single point were Blackpool, while Bolton were in 18th place. For both of them the death knell had not yet sounded. It would not, though, be long in coming as with the abolition of the maximum wage and dwindling crowds, their glory days were numbered. Yet of all the Lancashire sides who had known glory in the Fifties, Preston fell the first and the furthest. There was to be no occasional rally, no brief flirtation with the top flight before the reality of lower division football set in. The grind of matches against unfashionable League basement sides was about to begin.

Yet could this have been avoided? Tommy Thompson, for one, certainly believes so. "Tom Finney's retirement was a blow to the club and during the season there were a lot of injuries. After we went down, they got rid of a lot of players and it was the downfall of the club. They should have kept some of the older players on to get us out of Division Two straight away. We had a good youth team and they relied on that too much. Some of them made the grade at first-team level, but a lot of others didn't. From that day, the only way has been down. They are still today only in what was the old Second Division."

The loss of Tom Finney was undoubtedly a factor, as was the injury which restricted Thompson's appearances. Even so, he still finished as the leading goalscorer with 12 in all games, League, FA Cup and League Cup. He scored in a 4-0 win over Accrington Stanley in an FA Cup third-round replay on January 9, but would make only one more appearance for the club, playing in the 1-1 draw with Bolton Wanderers when North End's fate was already sealed.

The manager during the fateful relegation year was still Cliff Britton. He had been appointed in August 1956, but this campaign was to be his last as he was sacked in April 1961 and replaced by the trainer, Jimmy Milne. Britton had managed Burnley and Everton before his arrival at Deepdale. As a player he had represented Everton and England. In his early managerial days he was seen as a progressive coach who developed new strategies and training tactics. At Burnley he pioneered the 'iron curtain' defence that saw the side create records for the least number of goals conceded. In the first year of League football after the war, Burnley won promotion from the Second Division and reached the Cup Final, where they lost 1-0 to Charlton after extra-time. However, what had been new and innovative in the Forties was now seen as increasingly outdated.

Thompson said: "He was not very popular with the players. He was defensively minded and had a fixed idea of how he wanted the team to play. If the full-back went over the halfway line, he wanted to know what they were doing up there. He was also reluctant to spend any money. Preston had always been willing to go into the transfer market for good players. Now he was trying to scrounge a few players for nothing. Even down to small things he was tight. He would inspect the club houses the young players were in and set a limit on the money that could be spent on things like decorating."

Marian Bell echoes the view of many fans that it was the loss of Finney that made the difference. Certainly his presence was missed. It also underlines her view that the club were made to pay for an over-reliance on one of the greatest names in post-war football (to all Preston fans, of course, that should be THE greatest). Coupled to Finney's loss was the splitting up of the team. "That was the danger of relying on one man so much and having a first-team squad who all grew old together. There wasn't the experience to replace them and the players bought, well they took time to settle to the task. By then it was too late"

The season opened with three straight defeats and Preston blooded three new players for the visit of Arsenal with Peter Thompson, Alan Spavin and Tony Singleton all being given their chance. In the first half, North End created chances, but couldn't take them. They did, though, manage to keep the Londoners at bay with goalkeeper Else showing his First Division pedigree even if the team itself was shortly to lose its status. Singleton's debut came to an early end with a rib injury that reduced the home side to ten men for the second half. It was not to prove crucial as two late goals for Preston gave them their first win of the season. The first came when Kelsey, Arsenal's Welsh international goalkeeper, failed to hold a centre as he was challenged by Thompson and the other newcomer, Spavin, took full advantage. Two minutes later Alex Alston got on the scoresheet to make the game safe.

It was, though, to be a fleeting moment of glory as the general trend was decidedly unpromising and the form at Deepdale was, in the end, to prove costly. During the season they were to win only seven games at home. With only three wins on their travels, North End found points hard to come by. Hard though they tried, and despite putting on some spirited performances, the sad truth was that Preston were no longer good enough for the First Division. A slump of 14 games without a win began on October 22 with a 5-2 defeat at Upton Park. It included two defeats in each of which five goals were conceded, against Leicester City and Sheffield Wednesday. Then, just as all seemed doomed, there was a rally. It is often the case that when the situation appears hopeless, some of the pressure eases and the luck that has for so long been bad, suddenly changes and the breaks come your way. Only one defeat in eight games suddenly brought a glimmer of hope. Unfortunately, All Fool's Day marked the end of the revival.

Of all the grounds not to visit when the struggle was on for survival, White Hart Lane would have headed the list at this time. This was Tottenham Hotspur's double-winning season and relegation fodder like Preston were meat and drink to their star-studded line-up. To make matters worse, Spurs had faltered a little in the run-up to the Easter programme, with only six points from seven games, so any hopes that the Londoners might be in complacent mood were considerably wide of the mark. Spurs had beaten Chelsea 4-2 on their last outing. Now it was to be the turn of North End to be on the end of a pasting.

The visitors' cause was not helped by the reliable Else being missing between the posts and his deputy Alan Kelly contrived to present Spurs with a gift goal in the third minute when an innocuous shot slipped from his hands and trickled in off the near post. Nothing could have further undermined the Preston side's confidence more than to present a rampant Spurs with a 1-0 start so early in the game. Given the malaise in front of goal, which had stricken the forwards all season, that chances went begging was not a surprise. It ensured it was going to be a long afternoon for North End. They conceded five and it could easily have been more. Kelly was at fault with the third when he failed to hold a simple header to round off a particularly depressing day for the reserve goalkeeper. The only consolation was that on this form, Spurs would have been convincing winners against far better sides than Preston. It was the fifth time in the relegation season that North End had conceded five goals in a game. Their failure to score was also no surprise. They hit the net only 43 times in 42 matches and at one stage had gone six consecutive League games without scoring.

First-choice goalkeeper Fred Else had been spotted playing for Axwell Park Colliery Welfare FC while doing his National Service and joined the Deepdale staff at the start of the 1953-54 season. He made only one appearance that campaign, in a 4-0 win over Manchester City, and was only given that chance due to an eye injury suffered by George Thompson. For the next three seasons he had an understudy role before becoming first choice in the 1956-57 season. He stayed with Preston until 1961, when Blackburn Rovers paid £17,000 for his services. He wasted no time in getting into action, turning out for Blackburn in a pre-season friendly game against his old club on the day he signed.

While his rival Alan Kelly may have had a shaky start when he deputised for him at Spurs, the Irishman signed from Drumcondra in 1958 quickly established a reputation as a solid goalkeeper. Fortunately, his League debut, against Sheffield Wednesday in a 5-1 defeat that also marked the end of Joe Dunn's career, did not shatter his confidence and he enjoyed a successful career that was to last 17 years and include 447 League and 65 Cup matches. It established an appearance record that has not been broken. He won 47 caps for Ireland. After coaching and administration jobs at Deepdale in 1983, he was for a short time manager at the club.

It seemed the Tottenham result burst the bubble of optimism that had begun to convince players and fans alike that relegation could be avoided. There followed four games without a win, with defeats against Wolves and Aston Villa and draws with Manchester City and Bolton Wanderers. The situation was now perilous. For the penultimate game of the season, the visitors were Manchester United. Unfortunately for North End, the side sent out by Matt Busby were on a roll, having taken nine points from their five games since the

Easter break and they had scored ten goals in the last two games. The 21,256 crowd was swelled with thousands of their supporters who had made the short journey expecting another comfortable win. The portents were certainly not good for Preston.

A win at any time against Manchester United was something to celebrate. As it is today, they could afford to buy the best talent available. With victory offering at least a lifeline of First Division survival, the North End fans did all they could to raise the spirits of the side. It was United, though, who had the skills, tactics and confidence and it took only nine minutes for the Preston crowd to realise reality was about to shatter any dreams of an upset. Albert Quixall dribbled down the left and his accurate cross found Bobby Charlton whose shot was hard and accurate for the opening goal. Four minutes later it was two when Mark Pearson found Maurice Setters in open space and his shot beat Else. To make matters worse news trickled through that fellow relegation candidates Blackpool were a goal up at Birmingham. United eased their grip on the game and Peter Thompson, who was later to enjoy such a great career with Liverpool, led the Preston rally when he seized on a rebounded shot that ran loose in the penalty area. Garbutt Richardson brought the sides level with a header from a corner and the fans were again left dreaming that a miracle might be on, but just before half-time a Setters shot from a narrow angle on the right struck the far post and rebounded into the net. A fourth goal in the second half made the game safe and ensured Second Division football for Preston.

Tommy Thompson recalls: "The feeling in the dressing-room was not much different than usual after a defeat. A lot of us had been resigned to relegation. Everybody was doing their best. People were a bit down, but we were also trying to be positive and saying we were going to bounce straight back up."

A measure of the fans' apathy was an attendance of only 12,637 for the last game of the season at Burnden Park, although for Bolton fans who had seen their own side struggle at the basement of the First Division, a match against a side already relegated – even if it was a Lancashire derby – offered little interest. The game ended in a 1-1 draw. These were opponents who a few years before had attracted crowds of around 50,000 for some thrilling Cup-ties. The truth was that the quality of the new players now donning the white shirt of Preston was not of the calibre of a few seasons previously and those players with a proven record like Cunningham, Tommy Thompson and O'Farrell were nearing the end of their careers. Some fans hoped relegation would mean only a temporary stay in the lower division. A chance to rebuild and for younger players to gain some experience. It was not to be.

Hopes Of A Return Dashed

ANY hopes that Preston might quickly bounce back and win promotion were soon dashed as the worst fears of the fans came to be realised. Having brought the curtain down on the Preston careers of some great servants to the club, manager Jimmy Milne made barely a splash in the transfer market as he relied on the youngsters already on the books. Sadly, they proved unequal to the task of ensuring football in the Second Division was to be a temporary affair.

For Tommy Thompson, persistent knee trouble had taken its toll, but he still feels he had more to give the club he had served so well for five years. In the post-relegation clear out, though, he was not required and he joined Stoke City in June 1961. To show there was still life in the old inside-right, he helped his new club, who had re-signed Stanley Matthews, win promotion to the First Division in 1963 before ending his career at Fourth Division Barrow. On his return to Deepdale in the 1961-62 season he was made captain for the day and led Stoke to a 2-1 win. No doubt most of the 19,091 crowd were wishing their old favourite was still wearing the white of Preston as that game on March 3 coincided with an alarming slump in the home side's form.

He recalls: "Although there was pressure to end the maximum wage, it was still there. Getting rid of the older players didn't save the club anything. What did start coming in was some bonus money. At

Stoke we got £1 for every thousand on the gate over 12,000 and, given Stanley Matthews was playing and he was a huge draw, it was worth a few quid. There was also a bonus if we finished in the top three in the table. The basic wage, though, was £20. It was the same at Stoke as at Preston or at Manchester United."

Thompson was among a dozen players declared surplus to requirements for the start of life in the Second Division. A need to reduce the first-team squad and the spectre of the abolition of the maximum wage starting to haunt clubs may have been behind the decision. Dwindling attendances certainly didn't make the financial situation any easier. But fans couldn't help feeling it was a blinkered attitude. Others to depart with Thompson included Frank O'Farrell, Fred Else, Joe Walton and Joe Dunn. Their experience would be missed. For the start of the season the only new arrivals were Alfie Biggs, an inside-forward from Bristol Rovers, and wing-half Dave Barber, from Barnsley. Among the youngsters, one veteran remained. Willie Cunningham was still a force to be reckoned with at right-back.

Jimmy Milne was now the manager, but having been at Preston since before the war, first as a player and then trainer, he knew the players at his disposal. His feeling was that the youngsters could do the job and get Preston promotion. He was keen to give them their chance. If he had succeeded, history would have remembered him as a man of vision rather than the manager who led North End into football oblivion. He did, though, have the consolation of taking the side to Wembley in 1964.

Thompson said: "Jimmy was a popular figure and part of the fixtures at Deepdale. He was the trainer when I joined. He was all right but he never said much and I'm not sure what he would have been like as a manager. A lot of the problems he inherited. There should have been action taken earlier before we reached this stage. It is easy to attract quality players to a successful team. It is much more difficult when the team is struggling. A few years before we were a couple of games away from winning the championship. That was the time to buy. When Tommy Docherty left they should have replaced him with a top-class player. It was the same with others. They failed to appreciate what was happening."

Players given their chance the previous season were now to take on the responsibility of trying to get promotion and perhaps it was the pressure to do that which hit the form of many in the side. However, players like Peter Thompson, Alan Spavin and Tony Singleton would play a key role in the early years of the Sixties. They might have been plying their trade in the Second Division, but for a new generation of fans these were players who would enter the Preston pantheon.

Peter Thompson signed professional forms in 1959, after a spell as an apprentice at the club. Where once players could expect to serve a long spell in the lower sides, Preston's predicament, allied to the youngster's talent, meant that at only 17 he made his first appearance in the senior side and it couldn't have been a tougher baptism than against Arsenal in what proved the relegation year, although it was a bright start with a 2-0 win.

He would go on to win 16 caps for England, but not in the white shirt of Preston. The financial reality of being a Second Division club led to North End finally agreeing to his sale in August 1963, for £40,000. The former Deepdale legend Bill Shankly had seen the youngster's potential and there was no shrewder judge in the game. Liverpool beat off competition from Everton, Wolves and the Italian club Juventus to secure his signature. As well as international honours, he was to enjoy considerable domestic success, winning two League championship medals and an FA Cup winners' medal at Anfield.

Alan Spavin was from nearby Lancaster and arrived at Deepdale as a 15-year-old. He played in the side that reached the FA Youth Cup Final in 1960, where they lost to Chelsea. This side would prove a valuable nursery for the first team and none made the transition quicker than Spavin, who made his first-team debut the same season. He was the driving force in midfield and stayed with the club throughout the Sixties and up until 1973. The fortunes for Preston were largely depressing during his spell at the club, but he did have the consolation of a Cup Final appearance in 1964. He made 417 League appearances before playing in the North American Soccer League. His North End career, though, was not quite over as he made a further seven appearances on his return in 1977-78.

Centre-half Tony Singleton was another thrust into the fray as Preston's fortunes took a dive during the relegation season and he quickly made his home at the heart of the North End defence during the early to mid-Sixties. Having been discovered in local football, he was to play 287 League games. Consistent and dependable, he departed in the 1967-68 season as North End struggled to avoid relegation to the Third Division. Those desperate times, though, were still some way off.

In 1961-62 season, the club could manage only tenth place despite manager Milne realising once the campaign was under way that he needed more experience and dipping into the transfer market to secure centre-forward Alex Dawson from Manchester United for £20,000. It was a bid to guarantee some goals, after yet another poor start to the season with only one win in eight games – and that an away victory over Swansea Town. Dawson was a favourite with the crowd, who dubbed him 'the Black Prince' and plying his trade outside the top division, he was an effective striker, collecting 114 goals in 197 games. The first of those came on his debut against Rotherham United at Millmoor. He stayed at Preston until 1967 and a disagreement with the club, after which he had spells with Bury and Brighton and Hove Albion before retiring.

Despite his arrival, the results never improved sufficiently for North End to challenge Liverpool for the Second Division title, but there was the consolation of the Cup. A 3-2 win over Watford brought Frank O'Farrell back to Deepdale as he was now player-manager of Southern League side Weymouth. His return brought back memories for many of the fans for whom he was a great favourite.

Dense fog led to the first attempt to play the game being abandoned and it was a huge disappointment for the 1,200 travelling fans who had hoped to enjoy one of the non-League club's greatest days. When the game did finally go ahead the visitors, under the experienced tutelage of O'Farrell, ensured they were not disgraced and in the spirit of the FA Cup they battled hard and gave the home side a few anxious moments. However, once Dawson scored just before the interval when he headed home a goal-line clearance by a defender, the result was never in doubt. Six minutes after the restart, the tie was safe as Peter Thompson shot home.

It meant a fifth-round tie against Liverpool, which needed three matches to resolve before Thompson secured the only goal at Old Trafford to set up a meeting with Manchester United. A 0-0 draw earned Preston a replay back at Old Trafford, but in front of the biggest attendance the North End players witnessed all season – 63,468 – United proved to have the edge in a 2-1 win. Willie Cunningham had excelled throughout the Cup run but missed the United replay.

Cunningham said: "The great days were behind us and many of the players of the late Fifties era had now gone. Whether a few should have been kept for their experience is a good point. For players like myself it meant a lot of responsibility and I think we rose to it. I played some good football at this time, even though we were often not getting the results. There was always the hope that once the young side had settled, things would come right, but if we were to get back into the First Division it had to be quickly or we would be left behind with wages and transfer fees rising."

Hopes of promotion were soon thwarted the following year. Indeed, there was a greater danger of relegation with North End finishing 17th and winning only two games away from home. Such was their slump in form that there were some heavy defeats including a 7-1 reverse at Plymouth Argyle in the second match of the season. They were six down at half-time so the second half could be regarded as something of a moral victory. The side also lost 6-2 at home to Cardiff City on September 29. A 6-2 defeat at First Division Aston Villa ended interest in the League Cup at the fourth round while in the FA Cup, North End fell at the first hurdle, losing 4-1 at home to fellow Second Division side Sunderland.

Stoke City, boasting former North End favourite Tommy Thompson and the 48-year-old Stanley Matthews, would win the Second Division title and secure promotion. How the Preston faithful wished they could still call on some of the veterans their club had been so quick to part company with when relegation came two seasons earlier. Now there were fears that the unthinkable could happen and Preston would slip into the Third Division and football oblivion.

Between January and March 1963, Preston could manage only two games as football fell victim to one of the worst winters on record. The break, though, did not improve the team's fortunes and when football returned, the spectre of relegation still haunted the side, although they were to finish six points clear of the drop. Only one defeat in their last six games was a timely run of form that ensured League safety. On May 6, at Cardiff City, Willie Cunningham played his last game for Preston in a 1-1 draw. A sign of the future, though, was that in the following game Howard Kendall made his debut in a 2-2 draw with Newcastle United.

Kendall's talent was spotted while he was playing for England Schoolboys in a 7-3 win against Wales and he joined the club as an apprentice shortly afterwards and quickly made his first-team debut as the side struggled. He was only 16 when he played against Newcastle. A year later he would be taking to the Wembley stage in the FA Cup Final against West Ham United. England Under-23 honours followed and it was inevitable that he would part company with Preston as big-money offers were made. He moved to Everton for £80,000 in March 1967 with whom he won a League championship medal in 1970. He went on to enjoy a successful career in football management, much of it spent at Goodison Park.

It was a measure of the fans' frustration that there was a crowd of only 8,323 at Deepdale for the final game of the season against lowly Derby County, which the home side won 1-0 thanks to an Alex Dawson goal. The poor performances allied to the abolition of the maximum wage were now starting to hit the club where it hurt, in the bank balance. There was a loss of £13,141 recorded for the previous season and it would have been much worse but for the FA Cup run which generated a £21,278 profit. The wage bill was £43,892.

In a season of few highlights there was at least one game the fans could look back on and reflect on what might have been. On April

20, with no wins in any of their previous six games, the visitors were Swansea Town and a crowd of only 7,652 saw the home side for once hit form. The result was a 6-3 win, although it had started badly with Preston conceding a goal within a minute. The Swans did not enjoy their lead for long as in the sixth minute Alex Dawson fired home a pass from Peter Thompson. Against the run of play Swansea regained the lead when a Roy Evans free-kick found an unmarked Eddie Thomas.

A second-half fightback saw Dawson finish with a hat-trick. It might have been four had Glyn Davies, on the goal-line, not stopped a powerful shot with his head, but the defender paid the price, having to leave the field to recover. It clearly took its toll because the same player returned, only to put the ball through his own net. Davies must have dreaded playing against Preston. Four years earlier, he had been in the Derby County side that threw away the chance of a Cup shock against the Lilywhites.

Although it was to be best remembered at Deepdale for the FA Cup Final, the 1963-64 season also produced Preston's best season in League football to date since their relegation in 1961. It also featured a game that has gone into the records as one of Preston's matches of the decade. When North End fans gather to discuss great performances by the side, it is never too long before the game against Southampton on September 7 is recalled.

A reshuffle in the team saw six changes made by manager Jimmy Milne against a Southampton side who had turned The Dell into a fortress, having gone 21 games without defeat. That record was to be ended in a nine-goal thriller that Preston clinched by the odd goal. At half-time it was one apiece with a headed goal from a corner for George Kirby being cancelled out by Preston when Nobby Lawton was on target. Kelly in the Preston goal took a bang on the head that delayed the game for seven minutes while he was treated. Davey Burnside gave the Saints the lead again, but again Preston came back, this time a stinging shot from Dawson finding the net. The same player gave the Lilywhites the lead with 12 minutes left. There were, though, still four goals to come. Kirby's header from a corner again found the target. Kendall made a superb solo run to restore the lead. With three minutes left, a shot hit the crossbar and George O'Brien seized on the rebound. Four-all, but there was still time for Lawton to send the small contingent of travelling support home happy.

Such matches revived memories of great games from the Fifties and there were high hopes that First Division status could be regained. However, Preston finished third and were five points adrift of the promotion places finally occupied by champions Leeds and runners-up Sunderland. Who knows whether, without the undoubtedly welcome distraction of the FA Cup, North End could have managed to get back in the top flight? It was not to be that year and has never happened since.

Preston North End team in 1953-54, minus the great Tom Finney. Back row (left to right): Cunningham, Walton, Thompson, Mattinson, Dunn. Front row (players only): Campbell, Hatsell, Wayman, Baxter, Morrison, Marston.

Charlie Wayman scores against Leicester City in the 1954 FA Cup sixth-round first replay at Deepdale which ended 2-2. The Leicester goalkeeper is John Anderson.

North End fans wave to the camera before the 1954 FA Cup Final against West Bromwich Albion.

Charlie Wayman beats West Brom goalkeeper Jim Sanders to score Preston's second goal in the 1954 Cup Final. The goal stood although Albion players appealed for offside.

Willie Cunningham (far left) made 440 League appearances for North End after joining them in 1949. He ended his League career with Southport.

Joe Walton (left) joined Preston from Manchester United in 1947 and made just over 400 League appearances for the Deepdale club. He later played for Accrington Stanley.

Colourful Scottish international Tommy Docherty made 324 League appearances for Preston between 1949 and 1957. He was transferred to Arsenal, ended his playing career with Chelsea and then became an equally larger-than-life manager.

(Right) Preston North End's greatest player, Tom Finney. A tally of 187 goals in 433 League games and 76 England caps tell only part of the story.

Preston North End team, 1956-57. Back row (left to right): Docherty, Cunningham, Dunn, Else, Walton, O'Farrell. Front row (players only): Dagger, Thompson, Finney, Baxter, Taylor.

Tom Finney in action against Sheffield Wednesday in April 1957.

Preston's Sam Taylor (on ground) scores the only goal of the game against Sheffield Wednesday in April 1957. Finney, Curtis and Staniforth look on.

Tommy Thompson was already a prolific scorer when he joined Preston from Aston Villa in the mid-1950s. He scored 117 goals in only 188 League games for Preston before ending his career with Stoke and Barrow.

Flying Fred Else made 215 League appearances for Preston from 1953 to 1960, then served Blackburn and Barrow with equal distinction.

Tom Finney opens the scoring in Preston's 4-1 win at Ewood Park in October 1959.

Manchester United's Harry Gregg holds on to the ball as Alex Farrall closes on him in September 1959. United won 4-0.

Meet the Maestro. Tom Finney chats to young players at Deepdale.

Still pulling 'em in. A break from training for Tom Finney at Blackpool in January 1960.

Tom Finney leads out Preston for his final League appearance in April 1960. Preston beat Luton Town 2-0 to finish ninth in the old First Division.

Preston players link arms to sign *Auld Lang Syne* as Tom Finney says farewell to League football.

Finney in action during his final League appearance.

The stars gathered for Tom Finney's testimonial game. Back row (left to right): Jimmy Armfield, Nat Lofthouse, Alex Young, Bert Trautmann, Wilf Mannion, Billy Liddell and Bill Shankly. Front: Stanley Matthews, Stan Mortensen, Tom Finney, Neil Franklin and Billy Wright.

Two one-club men. Dave Sneddon and Joe Dunn training at Deepdale in March 1960. Dunn made 223 League appearances for Preston, Sneddon made 91. Neither played for any other Football League club.

Alan Spavin made over 400 League appearances in two spells for Preston.

Alan Kelly kept goal for Preston on 447 occasions in the Football League.

Sunderland's Jim Montgomery saves at the foot of a post as Alex Dawson comes roaring in at Deepdale in January 1963. North End lost this third-round FA Cup game 4-1.

Preston manager Jimmy Milne pictured in 1964 with his pet canaries.

Alex Dawson (left) began his career with 45 goals in 80 League games for Manchester United before joining Preston, where he netted 114 times in 197 League appearances. He later played for Bury, Brighton and Brentford.

It's in there somewhere. Action from the game against Manchester City in November 1964. Preston's players are Wilson, Godfrey, Spavin and Lawton.

Alec Ashworth and Alan Spavin put Portsmouth's goal under threat at Deepdale in April 1964. The result was a goalless draw.

Preston North End pictured in April 1964, shortly before the FA Cup Final in which they met West Ham United. Back row (left to right): Ross, Kendall, Donnelly, Singleton, Kelly, Davidson, Smith, Lawton. Front row: Wilson, Godfrey, Ashworth, Dawson, Spavin and Holden.

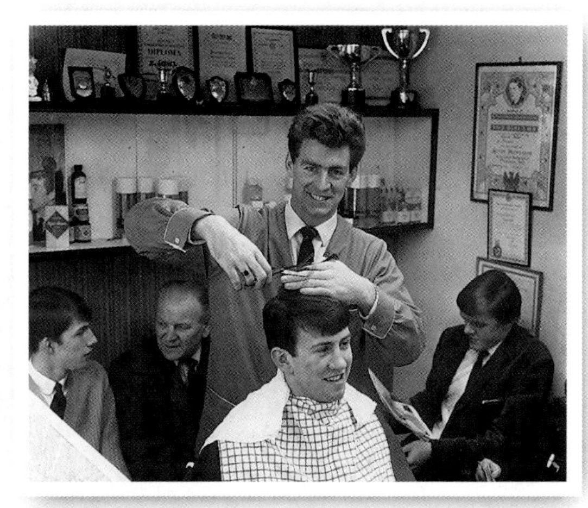

Goalkeeper Alan Kelly gives teammate Howard Kendall a trim.

Howard Kendall became the youngest-ever player to appear in an FA Cup Final when he lined up against West Ham in 1964. Kendall made 104 League appearances for North End before enjoying a great career with Everton. He later played for Birmingham, Stoke, Blackburn, Everton (again) and became a successful manager.

West Ham's Ronnie Boyce heads the winning goal of the 1964 FA Cup Final past George Ross and Alan Kelly.

Back To The Twin Towers

THE reality of football life in the Second Division was to be gloriously interrupted in 1964 with a successful FA Cup run that took Preston North End to Wembley and gave their supporters a brief taste of the good times they had so recently enjoyed. With each round successfully overcome, Cup fever gripped the town as the dreams of thousands were turned into reality by a team that were throwing the form book out of the window.

Cynics might say that the football gods were smiling on Preston when the draws were made in the later rounds, but a bit of luck is essential for a successful Cup run. In any case, the lucky charms failed to give Preston as many home draws as they would have liked, so North End faced a fair bit of travelling before they took the road to Wembley. And while there was lower division opposition later in the tournament, their two opening rounds were against First Division outfits.

A goalless draw against Nottingham Forest ensured a replay at Deepdale where the team made no mistake with a 2-1 win. The draw now produced a tie against old adversaries Bolton Wanderers. They were a First Division side, but this was to be their relegation season as the reality of the Sixties caught up with yet another of the East Lancashire clubs and sent them into decline. Matches against Wanderers would soon be a regular event as both languished in the Second Division and then even lower reaches of the Football League.

Bolton had needed a replay to dispose of Southern League Bath City, which raised the hopes of Preston fans keen to overturn recent history. The tie brought back memories of earlier epic Cup encounters between the two clubs. This was their third post-war meeting and a win would have been a hat-trick for Wanderers. The most notable earlier success was in their 1958 Cup-winning year when Preston were beaten at Deepdale in the third round. The following year, Wanderers also triumphed in a marathon that took three matches to decide.

Preston's cause was helped with Bolton's most experienced full-back, Roy Hartle, missing after suffering an eye injury while playing with his four-year-old son. The opening game at Burnden Park also saw the return of an old favourite in Doug Holden, who was now playing for North End after being bought the previous season in a desperate attempt to provide some experience during a spell of shocking results.

Holden brought some much-needed know-how to the forward line and the England international showed he could still perform at a high level and gave Bolton cause to rue letting him go. His first game for Wanderers had been as a 17-year-old and he holds the distinction with Nat Lofthouse of being the only Bolton players to appear in both the 1953 and 1958 Cup Finals. The first was famous as the 'Matthews Final' when Blackpool triumphed 4-3 and Stanley Matthews collected his winners' medal at the third attempt. The second was when Wanderers beat a post-Munich Manchester United side 2-0. Now his pace on the wing was being put to good use by Preston in the twilight of his career. He stayed three seasons at the club before emigrating to Australia.

The game was expected to be close and so it proved with Preston taking a two-goal lead through Dawson, but then with Bolton fighting back in a match that was in the great tradition of the Cup. Two goals by the oft-criticised Peter Deakin brought Wanderers level and earned a replay. The winners faced a home draw against Carlisle United, who would be that season's Fourth Division runners-up, and it was to be Preston who went through. In a game played at a terrific pace, it was the home side who went ahead when Dawson took advantage of a defensive slip by Bryan Edwards. Ten minutes after the break, Wanderers were level when from a corner by Gordon Taylor it was Edwards who got the header to make amends for his earlier mistake. The winning goal was scored by captain Nobby Lawton, who forced the ball across the line over Dave Hatton's falling body. Hatton was injured in the collision and it forced a reshuffle in the Bolton ranks with Francis Lee coming back into defence. In the game's closing seconds there was a scare for the home fans when it looked as if Bolton would equalise, but a defender cleared the ball off the line to ensure the win.

Around the same time that Holden arrived, another figure was recruited from a neighbouring club. This time it was Manchester United and the player was Nobby Lawton, signed for £11,500. Although he was not a first-team regular at Old Trafford and had only 36 League games for the Manchester club to his name, he proved a major asset at Deepdale. It was not just his talent as a player and his unbridled enthusiasm. The right-half also possessed great leadership qualities that saw him made captain. He went on to make 164 League and Cup appearances in his five years at the club before his transfer to Brighton and Hove Albion.

The success in the Cup continued. Carlisle United were beaten 1-0 at home and then a trip to recently-elected Fourth Division club Oxford United saw North End triumph 2-1. The football fates had been good to Preston, producing a succession of lower division sides in the later rounds. The balls came out of the bag well for the Lilywhites for the semi-final, producing a tie with fellow Second Division club Swansea Town, which was to be played at Villa Park. On the day, heavy rain turned the pitch into a bog and the decisive goal came when the sides were tied 1-1 and Tony Singleton scored his first goal for Preston with a 30-yard shot.

Roland Jessop had travelled to Birmingham with his young son. He said: "It was knee-deep in mud and hard work. It wasn't a great game, but Singleton hit this ball from way out and it went in. With the old heavy leather balls, such a shot took some doing, especially on a muddy pitch. I remember as a training exercise when I played local football we had to try to clear the crossbar with a throw in from the penalty spot – and there weren't many who could manage it."

He added: "One of the things the game did bring home to me was how far we had fallen. This was the Cup, so you play who you are drawn against, but Swansea were a Second Division side like us. Yet we had the history behind us. That was the worst part. North End had broken the record for transfer fees in the past and now we were just coming to terms with the fact that the great days were gone. It was to get worse. Soon we would be playing teams like Barnet and Wycombe Wanderers who were playing in the FA Amateur Cup when we were in the First Division."

Wilf Wareing had travelled down on one of the special trains being laid on for the day. He had queued all night for the ticket and now found himself in the ground with the rain lashing down. He vowed, though, it would be the last season he stood all night for a ticket for a big game. From the following year to the present day, he has been a season ticket holder. His first, in 1965, cost the princely sum of 12s 6d (63p).

The clamour for Cup Final tickets now gripped the town. Demand far outstripped supply and for every lucky soul who managed to secure a Wembley place there were many others left disappointed. It was 1954 all over again. Complaints about the distribution of tickets was again rife. Wareing was back on all-night vigil and he remembers the elation at securing the ticket. There had been a few thousand people standing there with him and he felt a sense of achievement at reaching the front and getting the ticket. Others were not to be so lucky.

Marian Bell recalls the Final brought more disappointment and not just on the field of play. She again missed out on a ticket. "They were like gold dust and again it was the genuine fans who missed out. For many people London was a great day out and a Cup Final was a social occasion. A lot of the real supporters didn't get a look in. I hate to say it but a lot of tickets went to the players and I think they sold them. I know it caused a lot of resentment in the town and many people were bitterly disappointed, including me. I watched it on the television and the result just made the whole occasion a complete disappointment."

Jessop was playing semi-professional football for Lytham and the club received complimentary tickets. Yet most of the players were Blackpool supporters so they took pity on him. Although the club held a draw for the much-prized tickets, all the players said they would give theirs to him if they got one and so he was on his way to Wembley.

He said: "It was a good game and although the result was disappointing, I thought we had played well. After the game a few of us went to Tottenham Hotspur's supporters' club and stayed until the early hours. At Preston we had just opened a club for the supporters and it was lovely, but I thought Spurs would have something that was the last word but it was a double-bayed house and very cramped. Still, it was a good way to spend the evening until it was time to catch the coach home."

For the FA Cup Final on May 2, 1964, Preston's opponents were West Ham United and the game proved one of the most entertaining seen at the Twin Towers. Too often the Final can be a disappointment that fails to live up to the hype as nerves and the desperate desire not to lose stifle good football. On this occasion both teams rose above such pressures to produce a thriller.

For weeks beforehand, the match was the talk of Preston. The players were taken to the Isle of Man for a break and to escape the mounting excitement in the town. Immediately prior to the game they stayed at an hotel in Weybridge. Manager Jimmy Milne was already suggesting to the press that there may be changes in the starting line-up for the Final and that Howard Kendall might play. Such news did not faze the youngster who reported he had slept well on the night before the match.

For the day itself, thousands wearing rosettes and black and white bowlers made the journey to London. Special trains were laid on and 100 keen fans flew from Blackpool to Luton. Many drove down the night before and slept in their cars ready for the big day. However they got there, all were sure of one thing: Preston were going to win the Cup.

Wareing recalls: "In the press, and I suppose everywhere outside the town, we were the underdogs because we were up against First Division opposition, but the team had been playing well and we had a good blend of youth and experience. I was confident we could win. There had been a lot of press interest in Howard Kendall, who was the youngest player to appear in an FA Cup Final, at 17, and we wondered how he would fare. We needn't have worried on that score."

He had caught the 7.10am special train to London and enjoyed the party spirit on the journey down with all the fans singing and enjoying a few pints of beer. As they arrived, the atmosphere was electric and the station was packed with fans awaiting the game with eager anticipation. Like many, he had a rattle with him and was giving full voice to his support for Preston. There were high hopes of proving the pundits wrong. Many recalled the disappointment of 1954 and the Wembley defeat against West Bromwich Albion. But there were a few with longer memories who shared their stories of the FA Cup win in 1938 and the George Mutch penalty that decided the game.

Wareing said: "We had missed out on promotion and I think everybody felt it was because the players were focussing on the Cup Final. Now we felt it would be only right if we could lift the trophy. Walking along Wembley Way, I was virtually carried along by the throng. It was wall-to-wall people. It meant a lot to us all, because for football fans there was no place like Wembley. At that time there wasn't the same opportunity to visit that there is now, with play-off games and such like being staged there. I must admit, the night before the game I hadn't been able to sleep with excitement."

After the presentation of the players, Walter Horan remembers thinking that Ian Davidson, the Scot signed from Kilmarnock the previous year, had been unlucky to miss out on the Final, having played in the first team in the run-up to the match, including the semi-final. There were rumours he had gone absent without leave shortly before the Final and that had been the reason Howard Kendall was picked in his place. He thought it might have been a case of Wembley nerves for Davidson. However, he was confident that the young Kendall would do the team proud. Because of his showbusiness commitments he was unable to travel to London and watched the game on television.

North End opened the scoring and sent the fans' hopes soaring. He remembered thinking another goal for the Lilywhites and the Cup was virtually won, but it was West Ham who equalised. Then with the clock ticking down, he feared the worst. Preston were to twice sacrifice a lead before losing the game 3-2 to a sensational goal scored with barely a minute of injury time left. It was to be a cruel end for the team that had belied their Second Division status for much of the game and, despite being a lower division side, had lived up to their reputation as a stylish football side. Certainly any neutrals, whose view was that North End were just there to make up the numbers, were well wide of the mark.

The Lancashire fans had waited only ten minutes for the opening goal. It was the perfect start to calm nerves. After good work by Kendall, a shot by North End's man of the match, Alex Dawson, was not held by Jim Standen in the West Ham goal and the ball was turned in by veteran Doug Holden. The early goal inspired the northern side and their hopes of being the first Division Two side in 33 years to win the Cup suddenly looked realistic. Yet while the Preston fans were still celebrating their goal, the lead was gone. Winger John Sissons raced down the touchline, cut inside and beat full-back George Ross before firing home a shot.

In this frenetic opening period there were further chances for both sides but it was the 40th minute before another goal was scored and it was Dawson who collected it. He met a Dave Wilson corner with a powerful header that left the 'keeper standing to ensure that at half-time, Preston had a well-deserved lead.

It lasted until the 52nd minute when a Geoff Hurst shot hit the bar and as Kelly in the Preston goal attempted to catch it, the ball spun into the net. With nine minutes to go, the Wembley injury jinx that often played a major part in the outcome of Cup Finals again featured. Kelly suffered a back injury. He returned after treatment, but was in great pain.

With many of the spectators preparing for extra-time, a 90th-minute goal by Ronnie Boyce, whose header converted a Peter Brabrook cross, ensured the Cup would be staying in London. Tiredness was taking its toll on the Preston players and West Ham were finding their rhythm and would surely have been favourites if the game had gone into extra-time. Afterwards both Alex Dawson and Doug Holden, who had played in five Cup Finals between them, were of the opinion that this had been the best. Certainly there was no disgrace in defeat. Managers Jim Milne and Ron Greenwood were both delighted with the way their teams had performed and the high standard of football. Bobby Moore praised North End for playing good football and admitted they had worried West Ham on many occasions. Among the neutrals, the game was said to compare with the great 1948 Final between Manchester United and Blackpool.

Wareing concurs, saying: "It was one of the best Wembley Finals with both sides playing good attacking football. It was a pleasure to say I had been there. However, in the last ten minutes we could see that West Ham had more skill. We were all over the place. They started to look like a First Division side. When it was over, some people were crying, but I thought we had been the underdogs and we had done our best. It was a great performance. Perhaps we just got tired towards the end."

He headed back to the train and there were celebrations as many fans took the view that the team had played well and they were going to enjoy their day out in London. They reasoned it might be a long while before they got another chance. They were to be proved right on that account.

Jim Proctor was working in London and had watched the match on television before finding a pub packed with Preston fans having a drink and he joined them. His view was that just getting to Wembley had been a terrific achievement and the build-up to the game and the match itself had been enjoyable. He was determined not to let the result spoil the night out.

The players attended a banquet at the Park Lane Hotel. The party was attended by Des O'Connor, The Vernon Girls and The Bachelors. After the celebration in London, there was the journey back to Preston. The team were given a tumultuous welcome on their return with an estimated 80,000 people lining the road as the players made a three-quarters-of-a-mile procession in an open-top coach with the Brindle Brass Band leading the way. At times police had to force a path through the mass of bodies keen to show their support for the team. The coach was reduced to a crawling pace through a town that everywhere seemed to have been painted blue and white for the occasion. There were cries of "We Want North End," and "Glory, Glory, Howard Kendall," from the crowd. As the coach passed Preston Royal Infirmary on its way to Deepdale, those patients who were well enough were brought into the grounds to see the team pass. Many supporters who had not been to Wembley planned to go to local cinemas where the film of the match was being shown again in colour.

When the coach reached the Town Hall, the players were each greeted by the Mayor of Preston, Councillor Cyril Molyneux, as they stepped out on to the balcony. He said: "They didn't win the Cup, but they won the admiration of the country." And addressing the players, he added: "You provided one of the greatest shows ever seen at Wembley. Thank you for all the glory you have brought to the town of Preston."

The Legacy And The Future

WITH the Second Division title won in the 1999-2000 season, the supporters of Preston North End were now starting to believe that they could return to the glory days in the top flight, and after years in the doldrums such ambition could no longer be dismissed as a mere flight of fancy. Off the field there were also clear indications that the worst for the club was behind them. Rebuilding work at the stadium was a visible sign of the investment being made. It was perhaps a reflection of the times in modern football that where a pie and a cup of Bovril were all the refreshments required on match days, the corporate catering at Deepdale was now under the auspices of the award-winning chef Paul Heathcote.

The food apart, though, any long-suffering North End fan will tell you the journey from the top to the League basement has been a nightmarish one, with little chance of glory to compensate for the disappointments along the way. Relegation in the early Sixties was not followed by a speedy return. As we have seen, the expected promotion to the First Division was never to be achieved in those early Sixties years, although there was the consolation of a Wembley Cup Final.

Instead, for Preston there has been a long road to the football wilderness, which culminated in a 23rd place in the old Fourth Division in 1985-86. Before then there had been some yo-yoing between the Third and Second Divisions, but no hope of a place back in the top flight. Such soccer luminaries as England World Cup winners Bobby Charlton and Nobby Stiles have sat in the manager's chair and tried to transform the club's fortunes, but to no avail. The nadir in 1985-86 saw once-Proud Preston applying for re-election to the Football League of which they were founder-members and the first champions. The following season they did at least have the satisfaction of winning promotion.

Tom Finney thinks that First Division football will be a testing time for the club, but he is delighted that everything is moving in the right direction. In winning the championship in 2000 he believes Preston were the outstanding side in the Second Division. Now there is the need to cope with better teams at the higher level. The chance to play sides recently relegated from the Premiership will give this Preston North End team a chance to gauge how good they are.

He added: "The problem with the Premiership is the millions it costs to compete in buying players and paying their wages. Teams like Watford and Bradford City got into the higher level, but it is whether they can stay there. Many who come down stay down. Watford couldn't stay up but they started the following season back in the First Division well. I think teams who cannot afford to buy big-name players have to rely on players who will give their all for the team. If the commitment is there, that can make up for an awful lot. Wimbledon survived season after season on team spirit and a never-say-die attitude, although in the end even that wasn't enough."

Finney knows that the support is there in the town and it is rallying to the North End cause. During the promotion season, Preston were averaging attendances of around 13,000. He accepts the reality of the modern age is that supporters will now only watch teams who are successful. The days of fans paying to see a side losing consistently are over. It was not the case in his day.

On a more general note, he believes there should be a greater use of wingers in the game. It's hardly surprising given that he was one of the greatest wingers football has ever seen. But he argues that if Brazil have still not given up the idea of playing wide players, neither should the English Premiership. "A lot of problems can be caused for defences when you have wingers with pace and skill able to go past defenders. Today there aren't the players who can do it and it means the space available isn't being exploited. Ryan Giggs at Manchester United is an exception and he shows what problems can be created for defenders. Now managers and trainers say they can't afford wingers and they have to have players who do more than wait for the ball all day."

There are other aspects of the game today with which the Preston president is not happy. Television has generated huge money for the top clubs, but it is largely being spent on players' escalating wages and it is not something he believes is good for the game. Rather he would like to see a greater proportion of the money spent on the youngsters coming through the grassroots of the game where the long-term benefits would be seen in improving general standards. The threat of abolishing transfer fees would also hit smaller clubs who develop young players.

Of course, Sir Tom Finney recognises that football has changed and comparisons with other eras are difficult, but he believes that although the game today is faster, it is no more skilful and there were more quality players at the top of the game in his playing days than there are now. Modern professionals do not have to play in the sort of conditions players were expected to turn out in during the Fifties, and the kit is lighter and better. The old leather ball has been replaced with the lighter plastic one which allows for longer-range shooting and greater control. Fitness and diet are more scientific than the old days when a training regime consisted of running around the outside of the pitch. He remembers even the England shirts all came in one size when he played.

A poll in the *Lancashire Evening Post* to find the best-ever Preston team produced a huge response and it comes as no surprise that the glory days of the Forties and Fifties are well represented. The highest number of votes unsurprisingly went to Tom Finney. Certainly there is no surprise that Alan Kelly is in goal and that two of the famous back line of the great years are there with high votes for Joe Marston and Tommy Docherty, with Howard Kendall edging out Willie Forbes. The veteran Willie Cunningham is one full-back along with a later generation player, Mark Lawrenson, now a television football pundit. The forwards include Alex Dawson and Peter Thompson, with two Manchester United legends sneaking in despite having forged their reputations at Old Trafford. Bobby Charlton, of course, who was player-manager in the Seventies. And the only player from the modern generation is David Beckham, courtesy of the five appearances he made while on loan in the mid-Nineties.

Wilf Wareing has been going to Deepdale since the Fifties and he now believes that the potential is there for North End to get into the Premiership. Who knows, he thinks, there may be players now coming through who will force their way into a greatest team poll. It is the first time he has felt everything has been right off the field since the Sixties, although the playing squad will need to be strengthened. "After watching them in the old First Division it is hard to imagine how far we have fallen since. Even when we were first relegated in the Sixties, I was not one of those who felt we would bounce back straight away. Sadly, I was proved right."

He added: "All the small-town Lancashire clubs declined at more or less the same time. Only Burnley held on for a while. The clubs just didn't have the money to compete with the big-city sides as transfer fees soared and the wages started to rise. Now, though, they are all starting to come back and Preston are part of that revival. It will take three or four seasons, but we will be back in the Premiership. Nowadays it is all about money. Even if North End go up, I can't see them ever challenging the top clubs for the title. Certain teams will always be at the top now because they can afford the best players from around the world. The best we can hope for is to emulate the likes of Leicester City and Derby County. We ought to be back where we belong, playing against the best teams and seeing the top players down at Deepdale."

He believes something of the old atmosphere of Deepdale is returning as the crowds are beginning to swell. After winning the

Second Division title in 1999-2000, the number of season tickets sold was more than 6,000 compared to the more usual 2,000. Towards the end of the championship-winning campaign, the crowd was often close to capacity. Wareing believes that the ground improvements mean the stadium is fit for Premiership football. What the crowd just need is for another Tom Finney to be discovered. That, of course, might be the impossible dream. Bill Scott wishes Preston well for the future and hopes they can return to former glories, but he is unlikely to be at Deepdale to witness the revival. He explained: "I have no great love of the modern game. Years ago a manager told me that if English clubs started copying the Italian style, it would kill the game. They did and it has. People don't want to see slow build-ups and sweepers. They want action and the full-back challenging with a winger and the centre-forward taking on the centre-half. There is nothing to compare nowadays with a Finney or a Matthews or a Raich Carter at their best. They were entertainers worth paying to see. Like most of us, they had all learned the game playing on cobbled streets. Not at some academy of excellence."

Willie Cunningham has also not been to Deepdale for some time, although that may change with the new management structure in place. It still rankles with the veteran who gave so many years to the club that, once he had finished playing, he was forgotten. And that was despite the fact that he lives in the shadow of the ground. Such a cavalier attitude to those who have been loyal servants of the club does, he believe, underline the malaise that gripped North End through the Sixties and Seventies. "I was never invited down, never offered a ticket and I certainly wouldn't go asking for one. To keep looking backwards is not a good thing, but neither is turning your back on the past. There was a lot wrong with the club in recent years, but hopefully that looks to be behind us now. Certainly I think the club can get back to the top division and compete. Whether it will be as good as the era I played in, I don't know. They were special times to be playing football."

Marian Bell is pleased with the new set-up at Preston. She believes the new chairman, Brian Gray, has brought business acumen to the club's off-the-field dealings, which has been sorely missed in recent years. She likes the fact that the club appear to be building slowly and steadily rather than over-reaching themselves with rapid expansion. Improvements to the ground as well as the team are welcome. She added: "We have a decent manager and some good players if we can hang on to them. One of the problems in the modern game is that the biggest cheque book often talks the loudest. Players don't stay at the same club and show the same loyalty they used to. Contracts don't seem to be worth the paper they are written on these days. In a few years I can see us playing in a 30,000-capacity stadium in the Premiership and, hopefully, I will be there watching. We need to avoid paying outrageous wages and over-the-top transfer fees. The club have to be a bit canny."

She recalls that after the war, the club acquired the knack of spotting future Scottish internationals like the Beattie brothers, Andy and Bobbie, Bill Shankly and Willie Cunningham. It is a talent the club needs to re-acquaint itself with to survive at the highest level. David Beckham played a few games in the mid-Nineties and scored two goals in his five games, but sadly he was on loan from Manchester United and they quickly grabbed him back.

"I am enjoying going to Deepdale more now than I have done for years," she confesses. "The facilities are first-class. There are seats, which is more comfortable, although I know some fans miss standing on the terraces. You get a good view and the football on show is good. In fact, it's better than it has been for a long time. And I think there will be more improvements to come. I now watch from the Tom Finney stand, which is an improvement and a suitable tribute to Sir Tom for all he has done. The Fifties were good, but I think having been down for so long, you appreciate the rise back up the League all the more. I've watched some rubbish since the glory days and we have had some inept people in charge. We had a series of Manchester United players like Bobby Charlton as manager and I can't tell you how bad they were. Now there are echoes of the Fifties team and there is some dignity."

After the dark days when only the real diehards bothered to go to Deepdale, Jim Proctor believes the worst is now behind the club and the future looks bright. Living back in the north of England, he is again a regular, but he hopes there will be more investment in a few quality players. The memory of Tom Finney and the players from the club's heyday still hang like a shadow. He believes the time is now right to look forward with confidence as well as relishing the glorious past.

However, Roland Jessop takes a more pessimistic view. He recalls a newspaper column, written by Tom Finney after his retirement, that has proved prophetic. In it he put the view that there would be a super league of around 11 or 12 teams and English clubs would fly to the Continent to play regular football against the best in Europe. The role for teams like Preston, Bolton Wanderers and Burnley would be as feeder clubs to provide players for the big-city sides. They would no longer be able to compete in their own right.

Jessop said: "Sadly, Tom could foresee the future and the fact that there would be no part at the top of the game for Preston. North End will never be a Premiership side. If we can keep our place in the First Division, then that is about our level. Even the Premiership is now a league of two halves. There are the big clubs with the money and the others just hanging on. I hope I'm wrong because the whole town is desperate for a successful team."

Walter Horan believes the club does not capture the imagination of the Preston public in the way they did in the Fifties and before. There are now too many competing attractions for people. And those who are interested in football are as likely to support the glamour teams as their local club. It is a trend he regrets. Seeing local youngsters wearing Manchester United shirts says a lot for the power of marketing, but is a sad indictment of the fortunes of Preston North End.

He recalls: "I remember when we won the Cup in 1938 we listened to the match on the radio and when it was over we went to the front door and everyone else in the street did the same. Everybody was smiling and waving and enjoying the moment. The win for the football team was something the whole town shared. Would a big win capture the imagination of the town in the same way today? The following season I was taken to my first match and saw a 3-2 win over Aston Villa. There was no thought that I would support anybody else but North End."

Now he believes the standard of football is nothing compared to what it was in the Fifties and the quality of the players has declined. He believes too many of the skills are being coached out of players and the game is played too much in midfield. In recent years, tactics mean less emphasis is placed on attack and so there are fewer shots, less goals and the game as a spectacle suffers. Of course, as the 2000-01 season got under way, there were signs that this was changing for the better.

The marked decline in North End's performances has also taken its toll on local loyalty, including his own. He has seen some dire matches at Deepdale in the years since the curtain came down on their glory days. In Preston's days in the League basement he remembers being asked by a local radio station to nominate his man of the match as the honoured guest. "I gave it to one of the Morris dancers who had been on at half-time. It got a laugh, but I don't think they were too pleased at the club."

Eddie Brown rarely sees North End play, preferring to concentrate on local league football where he still coaches and is able to continue having an input into the game. He believes, though, that the club has a secure future. However, he feels the legacy of North End goes beyond what happens on the field.

He explained "When my playing career ended after 16 years in the game, I was at a loss as to what to do when I was offered a job teaching at Preston Catholic College. The headmaster knew I had played for North End and I got the job on the strength of that. The football club has an important role in the life of the town. This was someone keen on football, looking after a footballer in his own town. I am very grateful for that. I later studied French so I could teach that, and I enjoyed 16 years as a teacher."

Tommy Thompson believes the play was different in his day but it was no less skilful and contrary to popular opinion the players were not slower. He believes few nowadays could match the pace of Finney or Matthews. What does happen in the modern game is that everybody is pressed into a small block. Two-thirds of the pitch has nobody in it. Good teams used to be able to dictate the pace of a game, but it is now all played at a frenetic speed.

Defenders stay behind the ball rather than coming out to make a tackle.

He added: "The behaviour of modern players is disgraceful when you consider the money they are on. They should be setting a far better example. Today's players have so much money and they buy posh houses and flash cars. They are isolated from the supporters. They have high profiles and are more like film stars. It was very different when I played."

Promotion to the First Division has brought back many of the derby games that were so enjoyed in the Fifties. Burnley and Bolton Wanderers again visited Deepdale in 2000-01. Tommy Thompson has played in the great Tyne and Wear derbies between Newcastle United and Sunderland and in his days at Aston Villa, the Birmingham derbies. He feels they are not the same today and fail to excite the passions they once did.

In recent years, a former Preston players' association has been formed and ex-players get together to chat about old times and take part in golf and bowling competitions. There are also sportsmen's dinners at which Walter Horan is sometimes persuaded to do a 20-minute slot. All are agreed that while the money may be better nowadays, they had the best of times playing in their era. They also hope that the good times are about to return to Deepdale and with the current regime, the pride will soon be put back in Proud Preston.

Index

Index

Index